Creating the

MANIA

An Inside Look at How
WrestleMania
Comes to Life

JON ROBINSON

Published by ECW Press
665 Gerrard Street East
Toronto, Ontario, Canada, M4M 1Y2
416-694-3348 / info@ecwpress.com

Editor for the press: Michael Holmes
Cover design: Franco Malagisi

PRINTING: FRIESENS   5   4   3   2   1
PRINTED AND BOUND IN CANADA

LIBRARY AND ARCHIVES CANADA
CATALOGUING IN PUBLICATION

Robinson, Jon (Journalist), author
Creating the mania : an inside look at how WrestleMania
comes to life / Jon Robinson.

Issued in print and electronic formats.
ISBN 978-1-77041-450-1 (hardcover)
ALSO ISSUED AS: 978-1-77305-271-7 (ePUB),
978-1-77305-272-4 (PDF)

1. WrestleMania (34th : 2018 : New Orleans, La.). 2. World
Wrestling Entertainment, Inc. 3. Wrestling matches—
Louisiana—New Orleans—History—21st century. 4. Wrestling
matches—United States—History—21st century. 5. Wrestling—
United States. I. Title.

GV1196.25.R64 2018   796.8120973
C2018-902588-3   C2018-902589-1

TABLE OF
CONTENTS

INTRODUCTION:
The Origins of *Mania*

Vince McMahon's unabashed aggression and swagger can be seen in everything he does from the board room to the weight room to the ring. The third-generation sports-entertainment promoter took control over the family business in 1982, with his mind set on growing WWE beyond simply the northeastern territories it had controlled for decades. With a focus on expanding WWE across the nation while transforming his company into a global brand, McMahon split from the National Wrestling Alliance in 1983, and, going against a long-standing tradition of promoters in the United States, started promoting shows across the country, holding events in other companies' territories while at the same time signing the best talent to exclusive deals.

"Back in the '80s, there was this 'Don't tread on me' philosophy," McMahon explains. "Quite frankly, all of the promoters were operating under a consent decree from the Justice Department because they had been colluding and continued to. Then I came along and bought my dad's business and decided I wanted to go national and, indeed, international with it.

"My dad didn't know that. Had he known that, he never would have sold me the northeast territory, which was his domain. All of these promoters were pretty rough guys. So when I began to compete with them, it was the first time they ever had competition. The idea was, you couldn't put your television show in someone else's territory. That was a no-no. Again, it was a collusion on the part of all those promoters. I came along and said, 'You know what? I have a better product. I want to compete. I want to go head to head with every single one of them.'"

And when Hulk Hogan joined McMahon in 1984, Hogan's bulging biceps and charismatic nature helped usher professional wrestling into the mainstream. McMahon's WWE stood at the forefront of what was quickly becoming a cultural phenomenon thanks to the Rock 'N' Wrestling storyline that featured Hogan alongside music megastars at the time, such as Cyndi Lauper. It was a story that was featured prominently on MTV, catapulting Hogan, McMahon, and WWE in front of millions of influential eyeballs who not only wanted their MTV but were now demanding headlocks, leg drops, and Hogan's 24-inch pythons alongside their Pat Benatar and David Bowie music videos.

"It was a natural connection," says McMahon. "In the '80s, rock was pretty wild. As Tina Turner would say, 'It's naughty.' So was WWE. It was a natural connection — a natural mix — and one that caught the imagination of a lot of people."

But McMahon wanted more than to simply be the darling of cable television. He knew that the MTV promotion would die out eventually, and for WWE to elevate to the level he envisioned, a level equal to that of sports organizations like the National Football League and Major League Baseball, he'd need to introduce a spectacle equivalent to the Super Bowl or World Series.

McMahon says the idea for *WrestleMania* first hit him while he was in the Bahamas. "I was actually on vacation for a couple of days,

probably the last vacation I've taken," laughs McMahon. "I was on the beach, when I dreamt up an idea: the Super Bowl is the culmination of, as it was at the time, the AFL and the NFL and, of course, you had the Emmys and the Oscars, and there was always this one big huge culminating event, whether it was sports or entertainment. So why not sports-entertainment?"

At the time, rival Jim Crockett Promotions featured an annual show called *Starrcade*, but McMahon wanted to take his show beyond mere moves in the ring by introducing the sizzle of celebrity, a move he felt would add appeal to mainstream viewers who might be watching his brand of sports-entertainment for the first time. The problem? How would fans watch? Before the days of pay-per-view, sporting events like the Indianapolis 500 and championship boxing were shown in arenas throughout the country, using closed-circuit television to varying degrees of success.

"It wasn't cable as we know it today; it wasn't PPV. It was in an arena, and in that arena there was a giant television screen and a projector. That's all you saw," says McMahon. "You paid your money to come to an arena and watch television. It wouldn't work today. It worked then but not for everything. It didn't work for the Indianapolis 500. It worked for boxing. They'd done a number of boxing exhibitions, so why not wrestling? It was a huge gamble. The biggest gamble I've ever been involved with. The roll of the dice. Because who knew that the WWE Universe would pay their money to watch television in an arena?"

But McMahon, always the risk-taker, decided to indeed roll those dice for his event that would become known as *WrestleMania*. To build up hype for the show, the WWE aired two wrestling specials on MTV. *The Brawl to End It All* showcased the tension between Cyndi Lauper and Captain Lou Albano that carried over from her "Girls Just Want to Have Fun" music video where Albano played Lauper's father. In the storyline, Lauper was offended by Albano's sexist attitude, so she decided to stand in the corner of Wendi Richter as Richter fought to defeat Albano's client, the Fabulous Moolah, for the Women's Championship.

After Richter won the title, Lauper and Albano reconciled, with Lauper even attempting to present Albano with an award, before the show was interrupted by an incensed "Rowdy" Roddy Piper, who ranted about the Rock 'N' Wrestling cross-promotion between MTV and WWE. When Hulk Hogan intervened to save the day for Lauper, it set up the second major show leading into *WrestleMania*, *The War to Settle the Score*, where Hogan defended his WWE Championship against Piper in the main event.

WWE was white-hot and fast becoming the talk of Hollywood as the company started attracting even more celebrities to sign up for *WrestleMania* appearances, including special guests The Rockettes, Liberace acting as a special guest timekeeper, Billy Martin serving as ring announcer, and Muhammad Ali serving as a special guest outside referee. The biggest addition to *WrestleMania*, however, was the inclusion of Mr. T in the main event as the television and movie star teamed up with Hulk Hogan to take on Piper and "Mr. Wonderful" Paul Orndorff inside New York's famed Madison Square Garden. Helping solidify *WrestleMania*'s spotlight even more was Hogan and Mr. T's starring roles in *Saturday Night Live* the night before the big show, as the duo hosted the late night comedy staple while shining the light even brighter in the WWE's direction.

But even with all of the mainstream media attention, people inside WWE's front office still worried about how many fans would show up to arenas around the country to watch wrestling on television. "We really didn't have any concern in terms of the number of venues that would show *WrestleMania*. They were available," says McMahon. "The only question was would it work? Would the WWE Universe watch television at an arena and pay a lot of money to do it? So it was a big-time risk. Acquiring venues really was not the problem. It was, would it happen? Would it be successful? I felt as though, obviously, that it would. As a matter of fact, I'd hired out the Rainbow Room, at the top of the RCA building, for a big-time party afterward, hoping it was going to be a success."

•

Inside the arena, the raucous crowd of 19,121 let McMahon and company know that *Wrestlemania* was a success, at least to the live audience who showed up to cheer and jeer the heroes and villains of the mat that fateful night of March 31, 1985. Action inside the ring saw Iron Sheik and Nikolai Volkoff become the new World Tag Team Champions, while Andre the Giant defeated Big John Studd in the $15,000 Body Slam Challenge. In the main event, Hulk Hogan and Mr. T defeated Piper and Orndorff after "Cowboy" Bob Orton interfered in the match. Orton, the father of current WWE Superstar Randy Orton, jumped off the top rope attempting to strike Hogan with the cast on his arm he used for years to cheat opponents, but, instead, Orton blasted Orndorff with the cast, knocking him out and opening the door for Hogan to make the pin. The crowd erupted for the Hogan/Mr. T victory, but behind the curtain McMahon was hoping for an even bigger win for WWE.

"After the event was over at Madison Square Garden, we began to get phone calls from the rest of the Eastern Seaboard about the closed-circuit numbers, and that too was a success," says an excited McMahon. "Well, we're on to something. What about in the Midwest? Chicago came in, that's working, and right on down the line all the way over to the West Coast. At the end of the night, we had been partying quite heavily.

"And with the success of *WrestleMania*, it really put us on the map and helped define who we were as 'sports-entertainment' before we even started using the term publicly. We asked ourselves, 'Okay, who are we?' Madison Avenue wanted to put a label on it, but we didn't want to say 'wrestling,' we didn't want to be 'pro wrestling' like everybody else. But how do we label this? How do we sell this? There'd never been a national vehicle, much less any television sales whatsoever. Because the thought was you couldn't sell wrestling. Certainly, when we went to a national basis, we proved them all wrong. All you needed was seventy percent of the United States and you had yourself a network. No one had ever had a network before. So how are we gonna present this to Madison Avenue? It can't be 'pro wrestling.' My dad was always more entertainment oriented than most of the other promoters anyhow. So hence, 'sports' in terms of the athleticism and 'entertainment' because that's what we do. *WrestleMania* had Liberace, The Rockettes, Cyndi Lauper, Billy Martin, Muhammad Ali. It was the kitchen sink thrown into what we normally do, and it caught the imagination of media all over the world. Never before had there been anything like this. That was the defining moment of what we know now as WWE and sports-entertainment. If *WrestleMania* had not succeeded, we certainly would not be where we are today."

Thirty-three years after that trailblazing event inside Madison Square Garden, *Forbes* now ranks *WrestleMania* as the sixth most valuable sporting event in the world, with a current brand value of $195 million, ranking behind only the Super Bowl, the Summer Olympics, the Winter Olympics, the FIFA World Cup, and the NCAA Final Four. And while *WrestleMania 1* was a single-day event, *WrestleMania* is now a week-long celebration for the WWE Universe. People travel from across the globe to get autographs at *WrestleMania* Axxess, there are Make-A-Wish events, the WWE Hall of Fame Induction Ceremony, *NXT TakeOver* (the flagship event for WWE's *NXT* brand), and, of course, *WrestleMania* itself, which has now grown to become a seven-hour event including the pre-show. In fact, from 2006 through 2017, *WrestleMania* has generated over $1 billion in economic impact for the cities that have hosted the event, while the WWE Universe at home has seen the broadcast change from closed circuit to pay-per-view to streaming on the WWE Network.

"*WrestleMania* is the be-all and end-all when it comes to sports-entertainment," says Bobby Roode, a 20-year veteran of the ring, who is now looking forward to participating in his very first event. "As a kid and as a fan of sports-entertainment, I watched every single *WrestleMania*. I can still remember being at my uncle's bar, sitting upstairs and tapping into an illegal feed just to watch the first *WrestleMania* on an old black-and-white television. I was a huge fan at that point, and to be able to say that I watched the very first *WrestleMania* is something that really sticks out in my mind."

And that passion for *WrestleMania* not only led Roode to become a Superstar, it led him to join WWE after years circling the globe for a variety of other wrestling companies.

"My dream, my goal throughout all my years in the business, is to perform at a *WrestleMania*. That's why I wanted to come to WWE," says Roode. "I would love nothing more than to be a part of this year's show in a big way. In New Orleans, in that dome, when my music hits and eighty thousand people sing 'Glorious' as I walk down that aisle — I see that moment as being the best moment of my life. That's something that I worked hard for and I dreamed about my entire career. Hopefully I can make the best of my opportunities as we head into *WrestleMania 34*. It would be a dream come true to be on that card. When it comes to sports-entertainment, it doesn't get any bigger than *WrestleMania*."

"And when it comes to *WrestleMania 34*, this is an event that will define careers," adds AJ Styles. "As performers, for everyone behind the scenes, this event is a year in the making. It's the single biggest show that some people will ever be on, so from top to bottom, we're all doing our best to make sure the WWE Universe witnesses a spectacle unlike anything they've ever seen before."

This is the story of *WrestleMania*, one year in the making . . .

PART ONE

2017

CHAPTER 1
Whose Yard Is
it Anyway?

APRIL 2, 2017: *WRESTLEMANIA 33*

How does it feel to have 75,000 people boo your every move? "Doesn't matter to me; I have thick skin," says Roman Reigns, after defeating WWE legend Undertaker in *WrestleMania 33*'s main event in Orlando to a chorus of hate usually reserved for the elite heels of this (or any) era. The thing is, Reigns, a six-foot-three, 265-pound former football player and second-generation Superstar, is billed as the next Rock, even if the deafening — sometimes mixed but often negative — crowd reactions are increasingly in line with him being the next John Cena, the athlete who served as WWE's main attraction for over a decade, despite not necessarily gaining the adoration of the entire WWE Universe. Leading into *WrestleMania 33*, the WWE Universe overwhelmingly booed Reigns, with only a few "Roman Empire" signs by diehard supporters scattered throughout the Orlando crowd. "It's weird because, in a situation like *WrestleMania*, it was almost like there were just two hundred people out there," says Reigns. "There can be so many people that it almost feels like hardly anybody is there. And then when you have a match and an opponent, you're so laser focused it feels like it's just you, him, and the ref.

"Obviously, you take into account the crowd, and that can help your flow, but when you can lock into your dance partner and just tell that story and you both get lost in selling for each other, that's when you know it's good. For me, Undertaker was such an opponent that once he made his entrance, I didn't see anything but him. Before he came out, I was looking all over. I was looking at the crowd, looking at the signs, just kind of getting a feel for the place; but then once his music hit, as soon as that gong went off, it was all business."

The match itself was a no-holds-barred slugfest that saw Undertaker chokeslam Reigns onto the announce table, only for Reigns to get up and spear his opponent through the Spanish announce table. The 23-minute match went back and forth and saw a series of near falls, including a devastating Last Ride and Tombstone from Undertaker, before a series of Reigns's spears took down the incomparable Dead Man. After Undertaker performed his signature sit-up, only to collapse, Reigns charged back and forth across the ring, then speared Taker again, leading to the Reigns victory, and (what looked like at the time) Undertaker's final farewell. After the match, Undertaker symbolically left his trademark gloves, hat, and jacket in the middle of the ring, then staggered to his wife (former WWE Superstar Michelle McCool) and gave her a quick kiss before walking up the ramp and raising his fist in the air to the deafening chant of "Thank you, Taker!" It was Undertaker's second *WrestleMania* loss in 25 years.

"I was sad that I was the one who had to do it, but I was happy that I was the one given the responsibility. It's such a weird emotion," says Reigns about being the man tapped to possibly retire Taker. "It's truly one of those deals where I was just like, 'Man, this should be the most exciting thing I've ever done, this should be amazing,' but at the same time, my heart felt so heavy because I've never cared for an opponent more than I did at that moment. I could see almost his whole career in his eyes, the weight that was on him every day of being Undertaker.

Having the streak, being around, and setting that bar — that's stressful, and you can see that when you work with someone of that stature. He has so much passion, so much experience, so much love for this business, and he carries it with him. And that's just what I learned from him: how to carry that every single day and to give as much as you can while at the same time living in the moment because you never know when it could all end.

"Not everybody is going to be as fortunate as Undertaker and have that long of a career. If I could have half as long of a career, I'll be happy. Just how aggressive this business is, how there's no recovery time — all of these bumps add up, and that's why there's such a respect for what he was able to accomplish. I just saw something about Joe Thomas of the Cleveland Browns, how he was able to play ten thousand consecutive snaps in the NFL, and that's the type of person Undertaker was to this business."

Reigns calls his time in the ring with Undertaker "a true learning experience," explaining how incredibly calm Taker is at all times. "He has to be the greatest veteran we've ever witnessed: he's seen everything, he's done everything, he's handled every situation," says Reigns. "I just wanted to take from him — the selling, his facials, the emotions — and just absorb what he does and take a page out of his playbook. That's actually what I do with every opponent I have. I try to learn from them, take things they do well, and take them for my own. I'm a very nitpicking person. Sometimes I'll watch the tape back and watch the way I walk, and it might just be one misstep, but that one little step will bother me.

"Undertaker has done it for so long that he knows every step. He knows exactly how he needs to hold his coat as he walks up the steps to how he gets into the ring with his hat. I watch all of that stuff. All of those little details add up, and it's all those little things that helped him become this big entity, this big superstar, this figure that will never be matched. I'm a lucky, lucky performer to have been able to see that, not on television, but five feet in front of me from inside the ring. I was

taking pictures in my mind so I could remember everything. That's just how I do it. I definitely learned a lot. It was just a one-time thing, but to be able to take what I learned from that experience made me so much better of a performer."

And while Reigns found the burden of possibly retiring Undertaker heavy, he already knew a year in advance the direction his character was headed: possibly retiring another legend. Everything after *WrestleMania 33* is about Creative building Reigns up to fight Brock Lesnar in the main event of *WrestleMania 34* in New Orleans. Lesnar's WWE contract is due to expire the night after *WrestleMania 34*, and if he doesn't re-sign in order to head back to the UFC, the main event against Reigns could be Lesnar's last match.

"It's an incredible situation that I'm in, a great responsibility, and it's one of those situations that they don't teach you," says Reigns. "They can't coach you for this. There's no class where they put you all in the ring and teach you how to main-event *WrestleMania* and retire legends. Nobody teaches you that, so I find myself in no-man's-land. But eventually, you have to go out there and perform and kill it or it's all for nothing. I'm looking forward to it. Regardless of how it shakes out, I look at myself as the main event no matter where I'm at, so I'm going to get it done."

To Reigns, being at *WrestleMania* is about more than the main event, however, as he sees the entire week as a reward for the nonstop work he puts in throughout the year. A reward that includes a week of much-needed family time. "There is no off-season," says Reigns. "We go fifty-two weeks a year, and when it comes down to it, this is the biggest live event of the year, the biggest gathering of people in sports-entertainment. What I'm so passionate about is we get to bring our families. For one full week, they get to be involved, they get to see it, they get to experience the event by our side. That's the tough part about our business: we're away from home every single week of the year. I've been on tour now for eleven, twelve days straight. I'm coming off of Hurricane Irma; my house was under water, and my wife is having to redo all kinds of stuff without me there. So that's the tough part of this job. That's the part a lot of people don't realize, that we have real lives, but we have to be here to keep the show going, which in turn helps our lives go. It's a weird connection, but that's what makes *WrestleMania* so special, so important, and so much of a reward and a celebration. We all have busted our asses for the past three hundred and sixty-five days, so for us to all be at an event that's bigger than anything we've ever been a part of and to let our loved ones experience it along with us, that's what is really cool."

But to get to that point, first Reigns needs to put in the work as he attempts to earn some newfound respect from the audience. "The way this business is built, with injuries, the stories and situations can get shaken up a lot," says Reigns. "For me, I try not to look too far ahead, I like to go program to program, but at the same time, I want to see the path, I want to know where I'm going to be on the big day. We can ask every talent in here, and every talent wants to be on that *WrestleMania* card. Someone like me, who has been fortunate enough to be in the main event for the last three years, there's only one place I want to be, so obviously these next few months are important. I'm going to work with John Cena so I can work my way back to the main event. I'm working a long program with Braun Strowman and helping to get him to the next level, but this is all a building phase for me. The next six months is to build me up so that I can take on someone like a Brock Lesnar. As far as how it all plays out — who knows? I pray it doesn't happen, but someone could get hurt and everything could change. It has happened with Seth Rollins, it has happened with me and my hernia in the past, and when it happens, it shakes up the entire card. You have an idea where you're headed, but you have to be willing to improvise.

"In the past, I've heard a full year's plan for me, but then it didn't end up happening that way at all," Reigns continues. "Sometimes it just depends on who your program is going to be with and how close Vince holds the plans to his vest. Sometimes you know: I'm going to be

with Strowman for three months and we're going to work our way to an Ambulance Match. Other times, you just don't know until you show up to the arena. Sometimes it's like, 'Man, what am I doing this week?' I might show up and beat up The Miz, but I'm like, 'What's the plan here?' So sometimes you really are just working week to week rather than knowing the full storyline months in advance. Not only that, but you have to take into account live events too, so we not only have our TV events but our live events, and all of those matches and stories are intertwined."

And if all roads do lead to Brock, Reigns is ready, as he wants to improve on the hard-hitting slugfest the two had back at *WrestleMania 31*. "Bret Hart told me that my first *WrestleMania* match against Brock was an instant classic," says Reigns. "At the after party, I was beat up and sore, because we just went out there and tried to out-physical everybody. There were a lot of great matches, a lot of great moments, big Superstars with The Rock and Ronda Rousey, but it was our match that everybody went home talking about. They saw our match and were like, 'Damn, now that was a fight.' When you're in the middle of it, you get lost in the moment and you feel like you're really fighting, especially with a beast like Brock Lesnar slapping you across the jaw. I was getting krunk in there, and I started to feed into my own self, and I think that showed, and I think that type of belief is what made our match so good.

"We are both athletes who can handle that type of physicality, and it's believable. We were able to go out there and tell a story, and it was a really simple story, so I don't think it will be difficult for us to top what we already did because now we can throw in a few different elements, a few different wrinkles. That physical fight, that physical brawl that you've come to know, that's just a skill set, and to me, guys like Braun Strowman and Samoa Joe and Bray Wyatt and Brock Lesnar, that physicality is something that you just can't teach. You can't teach a brother how to be aggressive, you just have to know how to do it, and me and Brock have that in spades."

As for the crowd reaction Reigns expects in New Orleans? "Hopefully really loud," he says with a laugh. "I've said it plenty of times, that's the only thing that matters to me. Make that noise. You paid that money, I'm a grown man, I have thick skin, so you're not going to hurt my feelings. I've been told a lot of different things throughout my life, and I've been called a bunch of things. Our whole goal is to get you outside of your regular life. We want to put you in our own version of Disney World for a few hours, and we hope you have fun and enjoy yourself, whether you're booing me or not. If you're there, do whatever you want, make as much noise as you want. You can boo me, but I feel good enough about my abilities and I know I can change things up on you at any moment, so I don't sweat it. I will take you on a ride, you just have to be willing to get a little nuts, get a little crazy, and get a little loud.

"Hell, it's New Orleans, hopefully by the time I get out there, they'll all be drunk."

CHAPTER 2

You Can Hate Me Now

APRIL 10, 2017: *WWE RAW*

The *Raw* after *WrestleMania* has become almost as anticipated as *WrestleMania* itself. From surprise returns to NXT talent making their *Raw* or *SmackDown* debuts to Money in the Bank cash-ins (Dolph Ziggler!), if there's one *Monday Night Raw* that's not to missed, this is it. This year saw the return of Finn Bálor, the debut of The Revival, and the announcement that Kurt Angle (just 72 hours removed from his Hall of Fame speech) would be the new General Manager of *Raw*. It was another announcement, however, that took the locker room by surprise, as Vince McMahon revealed plans for a Superstar Shake-up to take place the following week across both *Raw* and *SmackDown*, two days where the rosters across the competing shows would be changed on live TV. April 10 was the first night of the roster switches, with 21 Superstars changing brands across two episodes of action, including everyone from announcers to tag teams to power couples like The Miz and Maryse.

"What you saw on live TV, the reactions you saw from the Superstars who were changing shows, those were authentic reactions, because we had no idea," explains The Miz, a former reality star who has risen to the top of WWE, even being named *Rolling Stone's* 2017 Wrestler of the Year. "Nobody tells me anything. When we switched, that's when we switched. It was frustrating because I thought I did a really good job building myself up on *SmackDown* to the point where I thought I was in line for the WWE Championship. That's where you want to be. You want to be in the main event, and that's where I thought my character was going on *SmackDown*. Then, once you move to another show, you have to reinvent yourself because now there are new characters, new writers, new everything. So you have to prove yourself once again, and I feel like I'm the guy who always needs to prove himself over and over and over again, because no matter how good I am, no matter how great I do things, I will always have doubters and haters.

"And what people don't realize is switching from *SmackDown* to *Raw* is actually life-changing. *Raw* works Friday, Saturday, Sunday, Monday. *SmackDown* works Saturday, Sunday, Monday, Tuesday. So that switches up your entire week by switching up what days you're on the road. It doesn't sound like a lot, like it's only one day difference, but people have habits, they get used to doing certain things on certain days, and when you have to change up your schedule, you have to get used to everything all over again."

The Miz spent the previous month in a rivalry with John Cena, which had culminated in a Mixed Tag Team Match at *WrestleMania 33* between The Miz and his wife, Maryse, versus Cena and his longtime girlfriend, Nikki Bella. The match opened the door for the heels to openly mock and imitate their opponents on *Raw*. "Maryse and I did this thing we called Total Bellas Bullshit, leading into the match," says Miz. "About two months before *WrestleMania*, we were told what we were going to do, with all the weeks planned out. And we were told, 'Maybe you guys can mimic them.' But I was against the idea, I didn't think it would be good.

"But then Maryse and I were driving, and I was contemplating imitating them, and then I was like, 'This is how I would act,' all stiff like,

'Hello, Maryse, how are you?' And then she responded as Nikki and we just started riffing off each other, and then it hit us like, 'Wow, this could be something really good.' So we went back to the writers and we told them that we thought it was something that we could do really well, so they set it all up. There was nothing really written for the segment, we just knew we needed to hit a certain subject area, so Maryse and I just started riffing off each other and making stuff up as we went. We created this whole spectacle that helped make a match that nobody wanted to see into one of the must-see matches of *WrestleMania*. And performing at *WrestleMania* is the most incredible feeling, and it's a feeling that only a WWE Superstar or a person who is a part of WWE can experience. When you hear one hundred thousand people booing you or cheering you, there's nothing like it. People say they get goosebumps, and it's true — I've gotten goosebumps so many times — and that's why you keep doing it. That's why you put your body into harm's way. That's why we tell kids not to try this at home, because what we do is very, very dangerous, but we put our bodies through this because we want that reaction. To be able to look out at the crowd and to be able to play them like a puppet — it sounds terrible, but I can literally make a crowd cheer for me or I can make them boo me. I can do whatever I need to do to get a crowd to react to me, and that's the talent, that's what it is to be a WWE Superstar. We have the ability to control the crowd and give them a moment that they will remember for the rest of their lives. 'Remember that moment in *WrestleMania* when The Miz came out, I think he looked at me.' 'Remember when The Miz stole Daniel Bryan's "Yes!" kick and started using it — it was incredible.' They remember these things, and you hear about it, and it's things that fans take with them. It's absolutely incredible that we have that effect, and it happens every show. That audience pays their hard-earned money to see us, so we go out there whether we're sick, whether we're tired, and we work hard for the people so they can have that experience, so they can have that moment."

One moment the WWE Universe has been clamoring for is a

showdown between The Miz and longtime rival (and *SmackDown* General Manager) Daniel Bryan. Ever since Bryan debuted in NXT with The Miz serving as the longtime independent wrestler's mentor, the two have had heated exchanges, but nothing topped the live interaction the two had back in 2016, on an episode of *Talking Smack*. The two faced off in an iconic moment for both performers, a moment so raw it immediately led to speculation of an in-ring showdown. At the time, Bryan was out of action, still waiting to be cleared by WWE doctors before the two could get physical, a match The Miz still hopes will happen at *WrestleMania*.

Breaking down what happened during the infamous segment on *Talking Smack*, Miz says, "I have a lot of fans and a lot of haters. I was the Intercontinental Champion, and that day I was told I wasn't going to be on the show. They were introducing the *SmackDown* Tag Team Champions, they were introducing the new Women's Champion, and there wasn't any time for me on the show. Now this was coming from a guy who was just put on *SmackDown*, and they don't have time for me on the show? I'm the Intercontinental Champion. This is a title that I've always wanted. You look at the WWE Championship, the Universal Championship, and those are great, but when I was a kid, my heroes had this title, and they were known as the workhorses. They were known as the guys who could go out there with anybody and get it done. Even as a kid, I knew that. Shawn Michaels, Bret 'Hit Man' Hart, I'll even put Ultimate Warrior in there because he got a reaction from all crowds. As a kid, I loved Ultimate Warrior. I thought he was the best ever. He'd run out there, drop three clotheslines, hit the splash, and it was the greatest thing I had ever seen in my entire life. I'd paint my face. I'd wear streamers on my arms. And now I have this prestigious, most honorable title that had been just thrown down the toilet for the last ten years because it's the secondary title. But I don't want it to be the secondary title, I want it to be the main title because I want it to be the title that it was when I was a kid. I want it so you can have the WWE Champion and the Intercontinental Champion square off in the

ring, and you have no idea who is going to win. That's the type of title I want to make it, and they're going to sit there and tell me, 'Sorry, but we don't have room for you on the show.'

"So I went up to one of the producers and I said, 'Put me on *Talking Smack*.' He goes, 'Why?' And I tell him, 'Because I'm going to vent out all of my frustrations with everything that I have at this moment, and I'm going to vent it out on the General Manager of *SmackDown*, Daniel Bryan.' So I went up to Daniel and I said, 'Hey, man, I don't know how this is going to go, but I'm really upset,' and he actually gave me a couple of lines and told me maybe I could go here, here, here, and here. I told him, 'If you want to do anything, just go for it. I don't care.' I just wanted to make something captivating, something amazing. And when I went out there, I don't even remember anything, I just went blank. I don't remember saying any of the things I said. I was so angry and so mad and so frustrated, and I just let it all go. Sometimes when you're angry, you try to harness it, and you say to yourself, 'Calm down, calm down.' But in my head, I said, 'Fuck it, I don't care,' and I just started ripping into everything. And that's exactly what happened.

I lost it. I literally lost it on *Talking Smack*. I even told Daniel, 'If I say things that go too far, go ahead and hit me.' I didn't know if he was going to slap me, but instead he got up and walked away. And, honestly, him walking away was the biggest gift he could've given me. He gave me the power, and that's something a lot of people will not do. They'll stand up and get in your face so they don't look weak, but Daniel's just so smart and just so good, and we're such good foils for each other. When he got up and walked away, it gave me the opportunity to turn to the camera and just let loose on everyone."

But with The Miz's move to *Raw* in early April, it looked like the hope of an eventual Miz versus Bryan match would be scrapped for now, even if Bryan was cleared to return in time for *WrestleMania 34*.

"I'd rather not even know," says Miz. "I don't want to be told about some big storyline at *WrestleMania*, because you're fascinated, you're coming up with ideas, but then, two months down the line, plans change. Injuries happen; things just happen in WWE. We're live TV. We're not just a TV show where you can film it all in a day and then go month by month and we're ready to go. We're live. Some people get more over with the crowd in three months than other people do all year, so all of a sudden Creative is trying to figure out how to give that guy a spot on the card and how to best use him. There are so many pieces to this puzzle, and I'd rather not know until something is a definite and a for sure, and even then, in WWE, nothing is ever a definite or a for sure. I remember when I was part of the tag team champions with John Morrison, and we had a match that we developed, and we worked hard on it, doing things on the internet before the internet was cool. We were making YouTube videos before making YouTube videos was cool, and it was called The Dirt Sheet. And we were promoting this storyline, and we were told we were going to be on the show. We get to *WrestleMania*, and we're told, 'Sorry, you're moved to the pre-show. You're the opening match before the show even starts.' Literally, you can be told day of that you're not going to be on the show, so I'd rather just not know."

CHAPTER 3
The Modern Day Maharaja

MAY 21, 2017: WWE *BACKLASH*

Every morning, Jinder Mahal writes goals in his planner. Heading into 2017, Mahal wrote "Become a WWE champion." "I was undervaluing myself," Mahal says with a laugh. "I should've wrote 'Become WWE Champion!'" Mahal, who was released by WWE in 2014 and brought back in 2016 during the brand extension, had hoped to eventually contend for the Intercontinental or United States Championship. "I was fortunate enough to get a second chance," says Mahal. "After coming back, I took the opportunity to get into the best possible shape I could. I want to outwork all of my competition. I want to be known as the hardest working man in WWE. I want to be the most improved Superstar in WWE."

Mahal's impressive new physique and hard work eventually caught the eye of Vince McMahon, and when the opportunity to elevate a heel in the Andre the Giant Memorial Battle Royal arose, Mahal got the call. "I was given the chance, and I think I really stepped up," says Mahal, who found out about his *WrestleMania* rivalry with NFL star

Rob Gronkowski only hours before the event. The original plan for the battle royal saw Braun Strowman running roughshod through the competition, but when Gronkowski showed up to *WrestleMania* with longtime friend and WWE Superstar Mojo Rawley, Creative quickly pivoted direction. "The morning of *WrestleMania*, I had a signing at Axxess. I didn't have my phone on me while I was signing, so after I finished, I looked at my phone and I had text messages from everyone from writers to Talent Relations, and they were all trying to figure out where I was.

"Every message was, 'Hey, Jinder, where are you?' So I texted back that I was at Axxess, and they told me that I had to immediately get to the arena. They even sent a private car to pick me up, and by the time I got to the arena, the doors were already close to being open for the show, but we were able to quickly rehearse with Gronk before anyone could see what was going on. He had asked me during rehearsal, 'How hard do you want me to lay it in?' And I'm like, 'Just bring it full force.' It's *WrestleMania* and you only get one shot at it, and, chances are, this is going to be played over and over and over, so we wanted to make it look good. But he hit me so hard that I bounced back and hit the bottom rope — luckily, I was okay. His friend Mojo Rawley won, and it was a cool moment with the two of them celebrating, but, man, he hit me very, very hard.

"That clip of him hitting me went viral. It went everywhere. It was on sports websites; it was in newspapers. Gronk is a huge star and I was grateful that I got to work with him. It was amazing. My Instagram actually went up by fifty thousand followers after *WrestleMania*, and that show was something that motivated me personally."

Little did Mahal know, even bigger things were in store. "*WrestleMania* week, I saw [*SmackDown* Creative Vice President] Road Dogg in the hotel, and he told me, 'Hey, after *WrestleMania*, big things are coming your way,'" Mahal explains. "So I figured maybe I'd be in the running for the Intercontinental Championship or the United States Championship. That's all that he mentioned, so I had no idea I'd be elevated to WWE Champ so fast. After I got drafted to *SmackDown*, I actually had another encounter with Gronk in Boston. It was the first *SmackDown LIVE* after the Superstar Shake-up, so, of course, Gronk got involved and cost me my match again.

"The next week, it was announced that there was a Six-Pack Challenge Match to see who would be the number one contender. It's funny because I received a bunch of Tweets from people who were in shock that I was even in the match to see who'd be the number one contender. On the Monday, we had a live event before the Six-Pack challenge, and I was taping my wrists, and I was talking to some of the other performers in the athletic training room, and I was like, 'Who is Randy Orton going to work with? Is it Baron Corbin?' And they were like, 'Corbin's not even in the match; he's going to work with you.' I was like, 'What?' Then I see Randy walk into the training room twenty minutes later, and he tells me, 'Hey, I hear we're going to be working together.' So I thought it was just a one-shot pay-per-view deal. I didn't get any indication that I was going to be winning the WWE Championship until the actual day of *Backlash*. I had no idea. Once I got to the arena, they told me the plan, but like everything in WWE, I knew plans could change. So when I was walking backstage, I kept expecting someone to tell me things changed. Then I was in Gorilla before the match, and I was so nervous because I didn't want them to change their minds, but then I went out to the ring, and, eventually, they raised my arm."

The crowd inside the Allstate Arena was stunned as Mahal pinned Randy Orton to win the WWE Championship, elevating the former afterthought to the Modern Day Maharaja. "It was a great moment," says Mahal. "Coming back to Gorilla after the match, it was a really cool moment, because everyone was there: Vince, Triple H, Road Dogg, Michael Hayes, and a bunch of other WWE Superstars, including Drew McIntyre, which was funny, because three years earlier we were both released, and now we were both champions. Two of the three champions were now former members of 3MB who were released in 2014.

"Before I had won the number one contender, I would see Vince in Gorilla, and I'd tell him, 'Hey, Vince, one day I'm going to be your guy.' Vince saw that I was putting in a lot of work and that I was improving in-ring. I was getting in the best shape possible, and I had proven to Vince that I was responsible. When I was in 3MB, I don't blame them for not giving me any responsibility, because I was too immature. Outside of the ring, I wasn't taking things seriously, I wasn't focused, and, ultimately, it was my fault that I got released. It was my fault that I lost focus. But now, they see that I'm very hungry, I'm very motivated, and WWE is a place where they reward hard work. So I believe Vince saw the work I was putting in and ultimately rewarded me with the WWE Championship. I think they also needed someone to work with Randy right away. It was a situation similar to what happened with JBL when he worked the program with Eddie Guerrero for the WWE Championship. And actually JBL came up to me after I won the number one contender match, and he told me, 'The same thing happened to me. They needed someone to work with Eddie, and they put the jetpack on me.' So it was a really similar situation. I was able to work with Randy Orton right away. I was in the right place at the right time, and I had the right mindset and was motivated — I stepped up to the opportunity."

After the shocking victory, Mahal started studying tapes of past heel champions, drawing on inspiration from greats like Ric Flair and JBL in order to find ways to hang on to the Championship. "One of my favorites to study is Ric Flair," says Mahal. "Flair was the ultimate heel who always found a way to win and hang on to the Championship. That's the position I have with the Singh Brothers. By hook or by crook, I continue to hang on to my WWE Championship."

Mahal played the chicken heel role as planned, using the Singh Brothers to help him hang on to the title for far longer than anyone thought, including Mahal. But the reign enabled the new champ to travel to India on a promotional tour. "It was amazing," says Mahal. "I was there for three days, and, unfortunately, it went by in the snap of the fingers. It flew by. But we did so many cool things. I got to go to [the Michael Jordan of cricket] Sachin Tendulkar's house. I got to do a TV show. I got to do interviews and announce WWE's first-ever female Superstar from India. I had one public appearance at a mall, and I was blown away by the response. I posted the video on Instagram, because I was not expecting so many people to show up. Everywhere I went, from when I landed at the airport to when I left, I was mobbed. It was amazing to see. I never stood still, it was picture-picture-picture-picture.

"It's funny, because now that I'm traveling with the title, I've had to change my carry-on habits. I always keep the WWE Championship in my carry-on bag, I never check it. I always have the title with me. I know now that when I go through the security line, they are going to make me take it out, so I have this black velvet bag, and I just put the velvet bag and the title on the tray and push it through. A lot of times, the TSA agents want to take a picture. They don't realize what's inside, because it's a black bag, but once it goes through the scanner, you can see the look on their face. I was actually watching as it went through the scanner one time, and in the X-ray, you can see the big 'W' on the faceplate, so it looks really cool. Now, when I go to the airport in Tampa, where I live, the TSA agents all know me by now, and they're all like, 'Hey, champ!' And they're always very excited to see the WWE Championship. Having the title still gives me goosebumps. WWE even gave me a replica for home. What's cool is my original title had temporary face plates because I don't think the plan to give me the WWE Championship was made until the last minute. The original name plates are generic; they just say Jinder Mahal. But then they actually made new ones, so I got to keep the old ones, and I put those on the replica championship belt."

By October, the WWE champ made his *WrestleMania* hopes public, with Mahal officially challenging John Cena to a match at *WrestleMania 34*, even though his challenge wasn't cleared through Creative. It was like Mahal was writing down one of his goals, only this time in a public forum, hoping to will the match into reality. "It was just something that

I threw out," says Mahal. "I was doing a Q&A and one of the questions was 'Who are you looking to face at *WrestleMania*?' and I said John Cena. After that, I made the official challenge to John Cena. Why not aim for the biggest Superstar that there is? I want to face John Cena at an event like *WrestleMania*. That would really solidify myself as WWE Champion, and I think it would be a huge match, a blockbuster match. Cena is such a household name, and I've had a couple of matches with him, but I know a match against John Cena at *WrestleMania* would be amazing and it would be even more amazing if I beat John Cena at *WrestleMania*.

"I've been fortunate enough to compete at two *WrestleMania*s but only in the Andre the Giant Battle Royal. I consider myself to not have had that *WrestleMania* moment yet. I need that big singles match, I need that WWE Championship Match at *WrestleMania*. The year is such a grind with the travel and going from country to country, performing week after week, with no time off and missing family and having to compete on holidays and birthdays, but that one *WrestleMania* makes it all worth it. That's our reward. Just the crowd reaction and seeing the impact WWE has on people's lives, globally. The atmosphere around *WrestleMania* and the buzz around the entire city is just indescribable. It's a reminder of why we do what we do. You walk down the ramp and see the mass of people, and you get the biggest adrenaline rush you can even imagine. After the two *WrestleMania*s I was in, I was buzzing late at night, just lying in bed thinking about what had happened. That's why I want John Cena at *WrestleMania*."

Now, Mahal opens his planner every morning and writes his new goal: "Main-event *WrestleMania*!"

CHAPTER 4
Best for Business

JUNE 4, 2017: WWE HEADQUARTERS,
STAMFORD, CONNECTICUT

It's still 10 months to *WrestleMania*, but as *Extreme Rules* closes crowning Samoa Joe as the new number one contender to Brock Lesnar's Universal Championship, the behind-the-scenes business negotiations for the upcoming big show in New Orleans have already kicked into full gear. Back in January 2017, WWE announced that on April 8, 2018, *WrestleMania* was returning to the Big Easy, and since the announcement, John Saboor, WWE's Executive Vice President of Special Events, has not only been leading a coalition of WWE officials back and forth from Stamford, Connecticut, to New Orleans every three weeks to meet with city officials and community organizers, he's also been sitting in on the bidding process for future pay-per-views, including *SummerSlam* and the *Royal Rumble*.

"Our collective goal is to place *WrestleMania*, along with all of our big events, including *SummerSlam*, *Survivor Series*, and *Royal Rumble*, at least three years out," explains Saboor. "It has taken a long while to do that and a lot goes into doing that, but a three-year window gives us more than adequate time with our host cities and the local organizing committees. You'll hear us talk about them all the time, LOCs. The average planning cycle now is sixteen to eighteen months to bring together all the parts and pieces that make up *WrestleMania* week. Most recently, collectively twenty-nine events serve to make up *WrestleMania* week, and that's a combination of ticketed, community-based, and PR-based events. We now take enormous pride in the number of community-based events that we host along with our local organizing committee partners. Most recently, of those twenty-nine events, twelve of those were community based, meant to leave much more in the community than we can ever take out." Events range from Be-A-Star anti-bullying rallies to Special Olympics events to Make-A-Wish celebrations and hospital visits. "WWE as a company has put as much weight in our pro-social-based events as we do with our ticketed and revenue-based events, and that's something that we take an enormous amount of pride in," adds Saboor. "And I think it becomes another battle cry for a host city to use when they're evaluating whether or not they wish to deliver a formal proposal. Of that sixteen to eighteen month planning cycle, lots and lots and lots of that is spent planning these pro-social, community-based events.

"Winning the bid is one thing, but then the work really begins. I alongside others from WWE travel an average of every three weeks to our next host city, and we host LOC meetings, and the average LOC has between seventy-five and a hundred members representing every part of that community's private and public sectors and stakeholder organizations. You're talking an average of eight to ten hours of meetings during every one of those trips. It involves every part of WWE's business, whether that's television, consumer products, merchandise, community relations, marketing, PR, communications . . . the list goes on and on and on. It's a robust and comprehensive planning schedule that goes into building that blueprint."

And because of the staggering number of events WWE throws during the week, any city bidding to host *WrestleMania* needs to be deemed a "destination city" by organizers, where the WWE Universe

can spend their vacation juggling WWE and non-WWE events. *WrestleMania* moved from being a one-day show to a week-long celebration, and bidding cities need to understand the demand hosting *WrestleMania* brings. Back in 1988, WWE teamed with the Trump Organization to add autograph signings and even a five-kilometer run to *WrestleMania* week to help celebrate *WrestleMania IV*. Throughout the years, additional events were added, including an official pre-*WrestleMania* "Rage Party" televised live, March 27, 1999, the night before *WrestleMania XV*. In 2000, WWE added to the Superstar appearances and autograph signings fans enjoyed in previous years by introducing *WrestleMania* Axxess inside the Anaheim Convention Center, which included WWE Hall of Fame memorabilia, a full-sized wrestling ring, and the chance to commentate on historic matches.

By 2002, Axxess had grown to a three-day event, and by 2004, WWE relaunched its Hall of Fame Induction Ceremony to commemorate the likes of Big John Studd, Greg "The Hammer" Valentine, Sgt. Slaughter, Harley Race, and Bobby "The Brain" Heenan, coinciding with *WrestleMania XX*. "What is so exciting is that cities around North America are pursuing *WrestleMania* like they do the Super Bowl, like they do the NCAA Final Four and the NBA All-Star Game," says Saboor. "Similar to the world's great sporting events, WWE issues an RFP, a request for proposal, a bid document if you will, which is designed to showcase the history of *WrestleMania* and the opportunities for cities that win the right to host the event. Communities use the RFP as a guide post to create their formal proposals that they then provide to us for our consideration. That's been a major point of evolution over the past nine years. Not so long ago, *WrestleMania* was an enormously successful single-day arena event and worldwide pay-per-view. Today, it's not just a one-day event, it's planned as a week-long celebration and has an estimated 160,000-plus fans taking part throughout the week. So it became clear that cities were pursuing *WrestleMania* as an economic development strategy and we should talk to these cities like so many of our successful contemporaries to explain the opportunity, explain all that can be expected from a city, and give each city a true definition of what the week is and what opportunities it presents.

"There are so many factors that ultimately go into the overall decision, but primarily our decision-making process for the placement of *WrestleMania* is focused on identifying quality facilities and venues to host various WWE events throughout the week. We view that as the bedrock of any community's proposal. And then we evaluate a variety of other key elements including but certainly not limited to a level of involvement from public and private sector leadership; in many cases, this includes the city's chief elected officials, CEOs of corporations, and key stakeholder organizations — whether that's the city's sports commission or the city's convention and visitors bureau or the police department or the airport authority — who come together to help put the city's best foot forward. Input from that community's leadership is of paramount importance. Another factor is infrastructure available for the city, ranging from the airport to hotel rooms to transportation offerings. So important too is the city's past resume of hosting large events. Finally, which community will best embrace the vision for the continued growth of *WrestleMania* as our largest annual celebration. If that weren't enough, who is going to build the very best blueprint to welcome the world to *WrestleMania*. Most recently in Orlando, we had over seventy-five thousand in attendance at the Citrus Bowl, from all fifty states and sixty-two other countries. At WWE Axxess, which is our fan event and festival at the convention center, we had four consecutive nights of sellouts at the Amway Center, so we're talking over one hundred sixty-five thousand people who consumed the most recent presentation of *WrestleMania* week. So that host city has to have all of those attributes but also work very hard after they've won the right to host *WrestleMania* in building the blueprint along with our staff to welcome the world to *WrestleMania* week."

All hosting bids are heard by WWE's senior leadership team, including Saboor and Vince McMahon, with McMahon ultimately making the final decision. "Our Chairman created this celebration in 1985, and

Mercedes-Benz Superdome

this is our most important annual rite of passage," says Saboor. "He is still intimately involved in leading the discussion internally and making that final decision. But there is a large group of us who participate in making our recommendations. We review all of the formal proposals that we receive, then we pare that list down to a group of finalists, and the finalists are then invited to WWE's headquarters to deliver their proposals in person. Delegations are oftentimes led by that city's top elected official alongside participation by other teams of stakeholder organizations from within that community.

"It's never about who writes the biggest check. There are so many factors that go into the overall decision, but beyond the venues, beyond the infrastructure, beyond the embrace by the city's leadership, beyond all of the other factors, inducements, and incentives that we might consider, I think for our Chairman it has always been about measuring proposals by the sum of their parts and who will ultimately deliver the very best fan experience for the WWE Universe."

For *WrestleMania 34*, that winner was New Orleans, a favorite with McMahon and Saboor for hosting his grand event. "The WWE Universe has embraced the placement of *WrestleMania* in destination cities, and New Orleans is certainly no exception," says Saboor. "Beyond the WWE Universe participating in all that is *WrestleMania* week, they have demonstrated time and time again that they love to consume the entire experience. WWE has made a conscious decision to place our biggest annual celebration in a variety of destination cities around the country, and we do that for a lot of reasons. These are communities that put their very, very best foot forward to win, but *WrestleMania* week is offered as a family-friendly experience, and history demonstrates that generations of fans will converge on our host cities to celebrate this rite of passage. Moms and dads and sisters and brothers and grandfathers and grandmothers who all travel to these cities to take part and, in many cases, make this their annual family vacation. Whether it's New Orleans or Miami or Orlando or New York, these are cities that not only appeal in the strong history and heritage that they have with WWE, but these cities serve as very, very appealing destinations for the WWE Universe. So when we distill that back to New Orleans, what a great place to come and celebrate WWE's Super Bowl. What a great airport. What a great town. What a great French Quarter. What great hotels. We were there four years ago for our milestone thirtieth anniversary and the farthest walk that you had was between the New Orleans Convention Center and the Mercedes-Benz Superdome or the Smoothie King Center and that was fifteen minutes removed. And all along the way, there are points and points of attraction, from bars to restaurants to shopping . . . just everything that is the New Orleans experience. The WWE Universe told us with resounding passion that after our presentation of *WrestleMania XXX* that this is a city that they enjoy, this is a city that they wanted to return back to, and this is a city that they viewed as a destination. For us, it provides a powerful opportunity to match one of the most iconic sports-and-entertainment events with one of the world's most iconic cities."

As for the cities that lost out, Saboor explained that over 15 cities have bid to host *WrestleMania* over the past few bidding cycles. "We don't generally talk about the cities that don't win because at some point, they're likely to eventually win," he says. "We work very strategically to invite cities that we believe have all of the tools and resources necessary to host. We don't necessarily carpet bomb — these are very strategic decisions on who to invite into this process. As a result, we feel like at one point or another one of these cities will eventually host a *WrestleMania*, or now that we've built the opportunities to showcase our other major events like the *Royal Rumble*, *Survivor Series*, and *SummerSlam*, some of these cities will be selected to host one of our other major events. We don't talk about the cities that don't win, but we do talk about the number of cities that participate, and we work very, very closely with these cities to see which is the right fit. It takes a lot of energy to plan sixteen to eighteen months in advance, so I believe you don't pick a city to host just once. You're picking cities that can host multiple times because of the equity gained and the relationships formed with the city and its leadership — you hope you're making decisions that benefit you for many years to follow. Not every city that we send an RFP to is in the position to formally submit a proposal, but a great many do, and we're always looking for other cities for our other major events. An analogy might be, hey, there's not only the Final Four, but there are great NCAA regionals. And oftentimes, if someone doesn't win the Final Four, they should have the chance to win regionals if they have all the requisite tools and resources. At the same time, when you host the regionals, that trains you, that gets you more prepared to host a Final Four, or in our case, a *WrestleMania* in the future.

"I come from the other side of the table with our Chairman. I was part of our Orlando delegation along with Mayor Buddy Dyer that won the right to host *WrestleMania* back in 2008. We were a community that saw this amazing asset in *WrestleMania* and this amazing company in WWE that had been around for decades, but they really weren't going through formal selection processes. They were going to cities they knew through their decades-long live-event business, but they weren't really going through a process. We thought, wow, we can be one of the first cities to assign our political capital and our Good Housekeeping seal of approval and put our mayor on an airplane to go see a guy named Vince McMahon in a place called Stamford and talk about a thing called *WrestleMania*. We had the most amazing experience, so much so that I was sent to get it back, and the rest is history. I went to work for a company that goes out of its way, a company that takes enormous pride in consistently over-delivering for its partners. Orlando was no exception. For us, when I came to the WWE side of the table, we weren't selling vacuum cleaners. We are selling one of the world's most successful entertainment brands."

And the economic numbers that rolled in after *WrestleMania* 33 backed up Saboor's every word. Stats include $181.5 million in direct, indirect, and induced impact derived from spending by visitors to the Orlando region. $24.8 million spent on hotels and accommodations within Orlando, and among the seventy-nine percent of fans who were visiting from outside the region, the average person stayed 5.6 nights. Add to that the $9.3 million spent at area restaurants, and the numbers showcase why every year, the bid to host the event gets tighter and tighter.

But will *WrestleMania* ever see an international city win the hosting rights? "In the thirty-three-year history, *WrestleMania* has been held throughout North America, but with its enormous global appeal coupled with the incremental growth of the WWE Network, I can share that our Chairman and our senior leadership team is always viewing the potential selection of international host cities," says Saboor. "This is a global brand, and we're certainly conducting business around the globe currently, but we've only hosted *WrestleMania* in North America, and that was primarily due to the time zone and the pay-per-view model as it existed for a significant amount of time. I think the WWE Network does afford us some flexibility that potentially wasn't there before. I can say that these past few RFP cycles, we always keep top of mind these international cities. I think that we'll see during our lifetime some real serious consideration to some world cities to host this world-class event."

CHAPTER 5
Joe's Gonna Kill You

JUNE 5, 2017: *MONDAY NIGHT RAW*

Samoa Joe grabs the mic and says something not many men have ever had the nerve to say: "What stands here in front of you is a man that does not fear Brock Lesnar," said Joe, in one of his best promos of the year. "And though I hate to admit this, I'm incapable of fearing him because I'm far too envious of Brock Lesnar. You see, I want everything Brock Lesnar has, and I want to take it from him." These words brought Lesnar's trusted advocate, and maybe the best hype man to ever step foot in a ring, Paul Heyman, to say, "Brock Lesnar doesn't fear you either. . . . Samoa Joe, you are the worst-case scenario. Even if Brock Lesnar defends the Universal Championship against you, he's not leaving the ring the same way he came in, because even if Brock Lesnar gets by you, I know you're going to take a piece of Brock Lesnar with you. But just so you know, man to man, eyeball to eyeball, it's my job in life to make sure that at *Great Balls of Fire*, Brock Lesnar is your worst-case scenario. Samoa Joe, you want Brock Lesnar, you got Brock Lesnar."

Heyman extends his hand to seal the deal, but after the handshake, Joe backs Heyman into the corner, saying, "Your client chose not to escort you out tonight, and that's very disappointing, very disappointing to me, so I want to tell you something face to face, man to man . . . something very bad is going to happen to you right now . . . I'm going to wrap my arm around your throat and you're going to feel it tighten, you understand?" With that, Joe pivots behind Heyman and locks him in the Coquina Clutch. Both men drop to the mat, and Heyman begins tapping before finally being put to sleep by the Samoan Submission Machine.

The attack put Heyman, Lesnar, and the WWE Universe on notice: Samoa Joe is a supreme badass unlike anyone in the locker room, and the monster fans had watched for years running rampant on the independent scene had just been unleashed. "I saw that moment as make or break for my career," says Joe, whose in-ring career began back in 1999 but was always told he "didn't have the look" or "just didn't have what WWE was looking for." That all changed in 2015, when Paul "Triple H" Levesque signed Samoa Joe to an NXT contract, giving him his initial shot with the company before he was finally called up to the main roster in 2017. "In a sense, the moment with Heyman, the match with Brock, it was a do-or-die moment for me with the company. It was thrust upon me, and something I didn't expect. I heard that I might get the chance to work with Brock, and then they actually pulled the trigger. I think the first promo with Heyman, we knew we were on to something. Working with Brock let me show what I could do in the ring, and when they put you with Brock, you know they are starting to see you as one of the top guys. At the same time, you know you have to deliver, and I think if I didn't deliver in this match, in this build, that could've been it for me in WWE. That was my chance. The whole thing was a really cool moment, because being in the ring with Brock was one of my goals.

"But it was that first moment with Heyman that kicked off the whole thing. Paul is one of the last great orators of professional wrestling. He has the unique ability to show up, grab a microphone, and make any situation interesting. Even situations that might not seem big, Paul can start speaking, and he immediately captures the crowd. He's definitely part of the package with Brock. He understands the human mind better than most and he's able to tap into things with key words that make people emotionally invested in what he's talking about."

Lesnar and Joe followed that moment with some intense beat downs, including a wild brawl on June 15 that saw security and the entire *Raw* locker room empty in order to separate the two beasts. Joe kicked a restrained Lesnar square in the jaw before Lesnar launched himself into the sea of bodies for revenge. Lesnar, Heyman, and Joe went all-out selling for the upcoming *Great Balls of Fire* pay-per-view. "We definitely increased the pay-per-view buys with the build," laughs Joe. "So it was definitely cool for me. Any time there is a new pay-per-view, it's great because you can set the course for the future. For me, it was a great opportunity to be the focal point of the pay-per-view, and it enabled me to show my worth as far as trying to sell the product."

And the compelling storyline paid off big time at *Great Balls of Fire*, as Samoa Joe laid down one of the biggest beat downs of Brock

Lesnar's career, locking in the Coquina Clutch two times before Lesnar was able to turn the match thanks to a wild haymaker followed by an F5 to end the violent encounter. Lesnar won the match, but it was Samoa Joe who was elevated in the eyes of the WWE Universe and management. If the rivalry really was do or die for Joe's WWE career, he proved on one of the biggest stages of the year that he can main-event with anyone.

"Brock is an incredibly emotional performer," says Joe. "He comes out there with a lot of intensity, he feeds off emotion, and if you're not going all-out, he's going to swallow you whole. He's going to go out there and toss you around, and if you're not a hundred and twenty percent go-go-go when you're in there with Brock Lesnar, don't even bother going in the ring with him. At the same time, if you go out there and match intensity, if you go out there looking for a fight — and that's one thing that I've never had an issue with — Brock is going to go out there and give you his best. He definitely makes you a little worse for wear, but Brock is coming for a fight."

And a fight is just what Samoa Joe is looking for in *WrestleMania 34*. Looking ahead to New Orleans, if Joe could write the script, his first choice for an opponent would be Roman Reigns. "We bring out the best in each other," says Joe. "Roman's a very emotional performer too, and if you bring the heat, he can bring it back tenfold. If you manage to push the right buttons, you get something special when you're in the ring with him. If Roman's dance card is busy, I'll take Brock for a rematch. If Brock is busy, how about Braun Strowman? Whatever fortune befalls me, I'll be happy. We have a collection of giant mutant freaks who are at the top of the card right now with Roman, Brock, and Braun, and if I'm thrown into the mix, I'm more than fine with slaying dragons."

CHAPTER 6
Get These Hands

JULY 9, 2017: *GREAT BALLS OF FIRE*

Braun Strowman is pissed. The six-foot-eight, 385-pounder dubbed the "Monster Among Men" tore it up in early 2017 — including a dominant performance in *Royal Rumble* — but was left without a singles match at *WrestleMania 33*. To top it off, while Strowman was originally planned to win the Andre the Giant Memorial Battle Royal, the last-minute insertion of the Gronk storyline scrubbed those plans as well, leaving Strowman feeling frustrated backstage. "I was very disappointed," says the big man who rose from strongman competitions to compete inside the WWE ring. "I had been putting in a lot of hard work, and to be left out in the big dance, that struck a chord in me, and it's lit a fire under me to work harder day after day, night after night, show after show so that I can prove to everyone that I belong in the big dance and that I have what it takes to main-event *WrestleMania* one day, maybe even this *WrestleMania*, we'll see. It pissed me off that I wasn't a marquee match on the show, and then the battle royal didn't go as planned. It made me hungry, and this entire year I'm going to fight and claw for everything I have. I'm going to have a marquee match at *WrestleMania*."

Lighting the fire inside Strowman and inspiring him to do big things after *Mania* led the monster to have some of the most memorable and violent moments of 2017. April 10: Strowman overturned an ambulance on top of Roman Reigns. April 17: Strowman suplexed Big Show causing the entire ring to collapse. A week later, Strowman threw Kalisto off the side of the stage and into a dumpster. After suffering an elbow injury in May, Strowman returned on the June 19 episode of *Raw*, challenging Reigns to an Ambulance Match at *Great Balls of Fire*.

"Working with Roman has helped me tremendously," says Strowman. "He has really helped Braun Strowman come into character and show everyone what the 'Monster Among Men' is capable of doing. There's no one else like Roman. He is the single best talent in the world when it comes to sports-entertainment. We've been all over the world, night after night, and I've basically been in a rivalry with Roman Reigns since I debuted, and we've just been selling out arenas and putting butts in seats and getting smiles and tears and whatever other emotions we can evoke out of people. That's our job, and I really enjoy getting in the ring with him night after night. I know he has the same work ethic that I do, and that's to go out there and give one hundred percent of what he's capable of doing night in and night out, and it shows. He's the guy. Everybody wants to work with Roman. That's where the money is at. He's safe, so you don't have to worry about getting injured. He's going to go out there and put his body on the line with everything he does because he trusts you, and it takes a guy like that to be able to make the type of matches that we've been able to do. If only one guy is willing to go out there and work like that, it shows in the product, but when you have both guys out there putting their bodies on the line and giving one hundred, the proof is in the pudding. When we're on the card, people pay to see it.

"Flipping the ambulance was unreal TV. I've had an unbelievable 2017. Other than not locking down a marquee match at *WrestleMania*, I

can't complain. It's been one hell of a ride. I've worked with everybody and anybody in the industry this year. I picked up Ws against Roman Reigns. It has been the Year of the Monster, and I'm going to continue that into 2018 as we head toward *WrestleMania*."

Show after show, Strowman was delivering memorable moments, and he quickly became the most watched Superstar on YouTube, thanks to moments like his perfectly thrown office chair that squarely hit a running Reigns.

"Throwing the chair, the ambulance, the Fatal 4-Way, the turn-buckle that we broke. Sometimes, you do so much that it's almost like, 'Damn, what are we going to do next?'" says Reigns, as he talked about his rival. "That's how I think psychology wise — don't throw me into that turnbuckle tonight because we already broke one, so if we do it again and it doesn't break tonight, it's just going to look weaker, and we don't want to punch a hole in our own story. The stuff Braun comes up with is incredible. To have a guy six-foot-eight, almost 400 pounds — where do we even find these people? It's not like we can just go to Walmart. So whenever you have a situation like that, you want to make

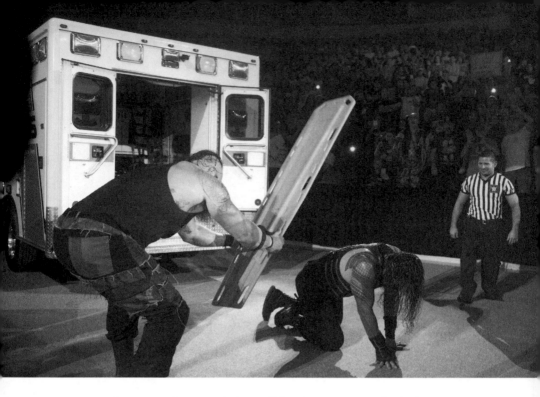

it special. He can do special things, like throw an attached chair at me. That's the cool part of it. That's the Disney World effect that this business has with some guys, and we need to continue to attract talent like that. Obviously, we need Braun Strowman to be Braun Strowman, we don't need another Braun Strowman, but we need another force to be reckoned with. We need another young stud thoroughbred like a Jason Jordan to step up. We have a lot of good talent, now it's just about utilizing them and teaching them. I've been blessed over the last three years with gaining all of this experience by being put in the frying pan, and, now, it's on me to pass that knowledge along. That's what I did with Strowman. I tried to teach him all the knowledge that I've gained and hopefully make him a better performer. That's what this generation is all about; that's what this generation cares about. We came to this place at a certain level, and now it's up to us to leave it in a better place than where we found it.

"When it comes to the chair throw, when I pictured it, I was walking around the ring and I asked him, 'If I try to spear you, can you throw this chair at me?' I was like, 'Just grab it and chuck it at me,' and

he literally did just that. And it wasn't like I was close, he had to throw it a good ten yards and he just winged it like a baseball. That just goes to show you his strength. That's not a gimmick chair. That's a real-deal office chair, and it's awkward to pick up, let alone throw with any accuracy. You don't find people like Braun Strowman who can pick up these chairs and chuck them across cubicles in the office."

Strowman admits to circling the arena before matches to play out viral moments in his mind before approaching opponents about the possibility of performing them on *Raw* or pay-per-views. Says Strowman, "Before I have a match, I actually walk around and see how the arena is set up that day so I can think of things that the WWE Universe has never seen before. I strive to do things that surprise them, whether that's throwing a chair at Roman Reigns as he runs toward me or flipping an ambulance. I try to take my performances one step further than you're used to seeing. I want to find that one thing that makes you go, 'Holy crap, I'm going to remember this match forever because Braun did this or Braun did that.' I take pride in figuring out little things to make the shock-and-awe factor go up to levels the WWE Universe just isn't used to.

"It's been crazy. I try not to get absorbed into social media — and it's hard because let's admit it, it rules the world now — but to see the positive feedback has been amazing. Everything I do seems to go viral. Everything I touch goes viral . . . whatever that means. I guess I'm *sick*. *Forbes* magazine did an article on how I'm the most viewed WWE Superstar on YouTube since April. My YouTube videos had over 70 million views in four months and the numbers continue to grow. Social media is an outlet that has helped push my character further than I would've been able to do without it. But really it's about those moments. When I threw the chair at Roman, it was a one in a million shot. We didn't rehearse it, we didn't do anything. When you try and pull off these big stunts, you always have to take into consideration how safe it will be, not only for the performers but for the crowd. Everyone sits so close, and we're larger than life human beings, so we have to take all of that into consideration to make sure nobody gets injured when we have these crazy spots."

Nine months to *WrestleMania* and Braun is on fire. Whispers of opponents are starting to leak, with everyone from Undertaker to Bray Wyatt rumored online, but Strowman advises the WWE Universe to believe the rumors at your own risk. "A couple of years ago, every rumor had me facing Undertaker at *WrestleMania*, but that was solely an internet rumor. I never actually heard anything about that at work," he says. "That's just all of the gossip on the internet. The WWE Universe likes to think they know what's going on behind the scenes, and there are reporters who like to report like they know what's really happening, but here's the thing: we're driving this car. We can tell you anything we want to tell you, and we can do a bait-and-switch on you in a heartbeat. We can make you think one thing, just to get you all mad about something, then we'll change things up, and fans are like, 'Oh man, this is what we really wanted.' Here's the thing, you guys don't know what you want. You hate one thing one minute, then you love it the next minute. My job is to go out there and either make you love me or make you hate me, and I don't care one way or the other. As long as I go out there and you're making noise, I'm happy.

"I'm just going to keep doing what I've been doing, and I want to find that moment that shocks the WWE Universe and shows them that I'm the next big thing. Without a doubt, I will be a Hall of Famer, I will main-event *WrestleMania*, and the Universe has caught only a glimpse of what I'm capable of doing. Keep your eyes open. You never know what I'm going to do next. Who knows, I might try to flip the ring out of the arena."

CHAPTER 7
Up, Up, Down, Down

AUGUST 20, 2017: WWE *SUMMERSLAM* PRE-SHOW

The New Day and The Usos are backstage inside Brooklyn's Barclays Center going over their upcoming match when word is passed down from Vince McMahon that he wants to change the ending sequence. "The finish for that match actually changed four times that day," explains The New Day's Xavier Woods (one-third of the team that also includes Kofi Kingston and Big E). "We finished figuring the match out, then they came to us and told us to change the end. We were going to win, then they switched to The Usos, so we figured out how to make it work, then they came to us an hour or two later and switched it back. Then, no joke, twenty minutes before we're supposed to go out, they changed the finish again.

"So we never actually know what's going on. It's not like Hollywood where you get a script, then you get three months to memorize it. You get bits of information, then you go out like two hours later, sometimes ten minutes later. Then there are situations where the finish of the match changes when you're already in the ring. They'll switch it

during the match, and you'll find out you're no longer winning or you go out there thinking you're about to lose, then they switch it and you'll be told during your match that you're going to win. It's a testament to everyone on the roster that we're able to ad lib, that we're able to do what we do and change things on the fly. It can be stressful, but it feels really good to be able to pull off a really cool, innovative match — something people really remember — that's given to you five minutes before WWE TV plays."

But The New Day and The Usos, as always, roll with the changes and turn what could've been a complicated situation into one of the most surprisingly brilliant tag team matches of the year. But the match being *surprisingly* brilliant is no indication of the talent level in the ring; it has more to do with the fact that the match was relegated to the *SummerSlam* pre-show. "We don't care where we are on the show, because our goal is to always have the best match possible," says Woods of The New Day. "We don't care if we're on the pre-show — if we're first, if we're last, if we're in the middle — our goal is that when the bell rings, everyone knows that this match is the best thing going that night. For us with The Usos, we were on the pre-show of *SummerSlam*, and we weren't upset, but we did have a chip on our shoulder: if you're going to put us on this early, good luck following us. I think the cool thing about this generation of WWE is that everybody has that mentality, and it makes the entire roster better, because if we're going out and completely obliterating things on the pre-show, once the show starts, those guys know that they have to step up their game too. And it works vice versa, when we see people go on before us and they tear it up out there, we know we need to make sure we're even more on point that night. Not that anyone ever wants to go out and phone it in, but when you see someone put on a performance that's really good, it hypes you up and makes you want to go out and be better. It's one of the cool things, like an unspoken rule on the roster, when you go out, you better make me work harder because I'm going on after you."

And both teams lived up to that billing, entering the ring with an innovative array of hard-hitting moves, including a Big E powerbomb of Woods onto Jimmy Uso, Jey diving off the security barricade, and Woods even ripping Jimmy's shirt before delivering a Ric Flair–esque chop. "If you had any doubt about the two best tag teams, you don't have any doubt after this match," said announcer John "Bradshaw" Layfield. And as sensational sequence after sensational sequence unfolded inside the ring, the WWE Universe showed their appreciation with chants of "This is awesome!"

"You go out there with expectation of getting a spot on that card," says Jimmy Uso. "So we went out there like, 'You're going to put us on the kickoff show, you're going to put us out there early, then we're going to hurt the show, in a good way.' We're going to go out there and make that match hard to follow, and all of us had that same mindset, The Usos and The New Day. And the rest of the show was hurt because the crowd already saw some fire before the official show even started. We went out there and we did the damn thing, and I'm happy

about that. You can put us on the kickoff, you can put us wherever and we're still going to work our asses off. We want to be in the movie, not just the preview of the movie."

"Here's the thing," adds Jimmy's twin brother and tag team partner, Jey Uso. "We've been having these off-the-chain tag matches. If you look at the resumes, we did our thing with The Shield, we did our thing with The Wyatts, so when it came to *SummerSlam*, we were really looking forward to tearing it down. There are two shows that my brother and I have never been on, one is *SummerSlam*, two is *WrestleMania*. Here you go, ya'll are going to be on the pre-show. What?! Okay, we have half an arena in here. If you watch it back, when we put that finish on them and get that one-two-three, there are people still walking down the aisle to get to their seats. They still have a full bag of popcorn. But we went out and had the best match on the show. *SummerSlam*, we did that."

The New Day and The Usos helped lead a resurgence of tag teams in WWE in 2017, something Woods takes pride in. "Leading the way for a tag team resurgence was always our goal," says Woods. "When we went to *Raw*, that's what we said we wanted to do. When we were on *Raw*, the tag teams were the best thing going, then when we went to *SmackDown*, we were like, 'Okay, let's help build up the tag teams here.' A few months later, I feel like the *SmackDown* tag team division is the best thing going on WWE television. Everybody knows once the bell rings, you're going to see one hell of a match, no matter who the two teams are.

"With all of the stuff that we've done, The New Day has a little bit of a longer leash than other people. There's some crazy stuff that we're able to get away with, so rather than keep it all to ourselves, we like to spread the wealth throughout the division. We have The New Day, we have The Usos on the come-up really heavy, and now we have Rusev and English and Shelton and Gable. We've been able to spread the spotlight around, give these guys opportunities, and that not only helps us as The New Day, but it also helps the entire division. For example, at

Clash of Champions, we put Gable in the spotlight, where he looked like he was the man. If people connect more with Gable and Shelton, when we work with them, the matches are going to be more intense because people will care about them more. We have no problem taking the backseat in a match in order to give somebody else the spotlight because if somebody else can shine, then it's the entire division that's growing. It's a rising-tide-lifts-all-boats type of situation."

"When they first came to *SmackDown*, I was excited because we ran with The New Day before, so we knew what to expect," says Jey Uso. "There's just an unspoken language where we can go in there and just vibe. We know we're going to tear the roof off this place. It's fun, it's new, and I got to feel it. If I feel it, and the team across from me feels it, and we have that energy every night, we could light the Universe on fire. It just kept getting better and better and better every single pay-per-view. Every time we went out, the goal was to top the last one, and we had that mindset every single time. My hats off to The New Day. I love them boys. I'm proud of them and the type of work that we put on."

"When the brand split, we knew we were a tag team on *SmackDown*, and now The New Day was coming over as well, so there was already competition between us, and we wanted to show everyone what we could do," adds Jimmy. "The last time there was a hot angle between two tag teams like this, it was back in the Attitude Era with The Dudley Boyz, Edge and Christian, and The Hardy Boyz. And that's what we grew up on. We grew up on tag team wrestling, so when The New Day came over here to *SmackDown*, we finally got the dance partners we were looking for, and we knew we were going to make it really hard for any act to follow. There ain't nothing like The New Day and The Usos rivalry."

But not everything came up championships and pancakes for The New Day. When the group first debuted back in 2014, the three-man stable showcased a gospel gimmick that was immediately panned by critics and met with a chorus of boos from the *Raw* audience. But the more distance the talented trio put between themselves and the awful

gospel stereotypes, and the more they focused on creating their own identity — complete with the introduction of Francesca the Trombone, an instrument Woods plays throughout their entrance and utilizes during matches — Woods, Big E, and Kofi Kingston soon became one of the most popular teams of the last decade.

"I went to E and told him this idea I had for a group," says Woods. "But we had some stuff to figure out because we weren't clicking together as a tag team the way we wanted to. I figured we needed a third member, so I thought about it for a week or two, and at the time, Kofi wasn't really doing anything, and I thought he might be a good fit with us. So we presented him with the idea and he liked it, so we just started spending a lot of time together, trying to figure out how to make stuff work. Before people saw us together on TV, we had been together backstage for about eight months, so it's not something that just came out of nowhere. It developed slowly over time.

"What helped us get this far is we never work for an individual. We didn't go into this to be selfish. We realized right away that if the group succeeds, we all succeed. That's actually the downfall of a lot of teams and groups, and that's not just in wrestling but in general. Our unselfishness and our willingness to do everything for the team is the main reason we've been so successful so far."

And it's because of the group's success that Woods claims he will call it quits on his career if he's ever separated from The New Day. "I love being in The New Day," explains Woods. "I love being in a tag team. That's what I want to do. I have no desire to perform inside of a ring unless it's as part of The New Day. Once The New Day is done, I'm done. I will never have this much fun again in wrestling, and if I'm not having this much fun at my job, then I don't think I need to be doing this job, and I think it's the same for Kofi and E."

And while The New Day played the roles of hosts for *WrestleMania 33*, the trio is calling for a match against The Usos in New Orleans. "We kicked around some ideas with them, but we want something where all three of us can be in the match. Some sort of six-man involving the

Usos and a partner of their choice. Maybe a TLC Match with them where we can go out and show out."

Tables, Ladders, and Chairs Match against The Usos? Jimmy and Jey are down. "It's been three-on-two all year, they might as well make it a Handicap Match," laughs Jey. "We don't care. We don't need a partner."

Adds Jimmy, "At this point, we deserve to be on the main card at *WrestleMania 34* in New Orleans. We lifted the whole year up, we've been killing it on every pay-per-view, and, dammit, you might as well call us the pay-per-view killers because if you put us on that card, you're going to get your money's worth. You're going to get a hell of a match between The Usos and whoever the hell it is, especially if it's The New Day. We deserve to be on that card."

CHAPTER 8
Sierra. Hotel. India. Echo. Lima. Delta.

AUGUST 20, 2017: WWE *SUMMERSLAM*

SummerSlam was headlined by Brock Lesnar defending the Universal Championship against Roman Reigns, Samoa Joe, and Braun Strowman in a Fatal 4-Way. While The New Day and The Usos did their best to steal the show, one of the most talked-about matches of the weekend was the reunited Seth Rollins and Dean Ambrose (two-thirds of The Shield) defeating Cesaro and Sheamus, aka The Bar, for the WWE Tag Team Championship. This should come as no surprise, though, as 2017 was the year of the tag team as The Usos, The New Day, The Bar, The Hardy Boyz, Shelton Benjamin and Chad Gable, Rusev and English, The Revival, Luke Gallows and Karl Anderson, and The Fashion Police put on consistently great matches and backstage moments of anybody on the roster.

But it was the eagerly awaited reunion of Rollins and Ambrose (leading to a later reunion with Reigns) that left the WWE Universe buzzing long after the show was over.

"It's definitely a thing people made clear that they wanted to see. They've been asking about it everywhere we went: 'When is The Shield getting back together?'" says Ambrose. "It's electric to see us together. People didn't think they'd ever see it again. They didn't think Seth and I would reconcile and form a partnership again. In Boston, it was the loudest reaction you'll ever hear for two guys bumping fists together."

Rollins agrees: "Everyone wanted to see a Shield reunion, and when Ambrose came over from *SmackDown*, we all realized that this could be a possibility, that there could be a reconciliation, but we didn't know when it was going to happen or where everybody's stories were going to fall. But we found a good time toward the end of the year to make peace with each other, and the WWE Universe is super excited. We've seen a ton of the new Shield shirts at live events and the response has been really positive. It has been a cool experience for me and for the fans who have been asking for this reunion to happen for the last three years."

Inside the ring, Rollins and Ambrose clicked at *SummerSlam*, like the team never broke up, defeating The Bar in an instant classic that left the crowd breathless. "It's all about one-upmanship," Rollins says about The Shield's rivalry with Cesaro and Sheamus. "They fancy themselves as two of the best in the world, and Ambrose and I feel the same way. Sheamus and Cesaro have been together now for almost a year as The Bar, and they really perfected what they do as two big strong world-beaters. And Ambrose and I, we're all around technicians and brawlers and highflyers, and we think we're the best team in the world, so when push comes to shove, we go out there and try to outdo each other. It's like one of those situations where we're going to make them better and they're going to make us better, and by putting us together, it really brings out the best in all four of us. On top of that, we're on a show where we're not the main event, and it's kind of annoying to us. All four of us have the mindset that we should be the main event, so when we're first on the card or sandwiched between two supposedly bigger matches, we want to make everyone after us work harder, so we go out there and we give it our best effort every single night. Think about the pay-per-view match that we had on *No Mercy* with the iconic image of Cesaro's bloody mouth after the slingshot in the corner, then add in *SummerSlam* and the *Raw* matches we had and the TLC Match, and this rivalry speaks for itself."

"Cesaro and Sheamus are two of the most experienced, two of the top guys here, but I feel like once Seth and I became a team, we instantly became the best tag team in the world," adds Ambrose. "That's just how I feel, whether it's true or not. Our ability to work together is better than anybody else in the world. It's just part of our cocky mentality, call it confidence or whatever, but that's what makes The Shield. We'll walk into a ring full of twenty guys, and it's just the three of us, but we know we're going to win. That's not smart, but that's how we do it. But what I will say is that The Bar is a close number two tag team in the world. They work together so exceptionally, and they match up with us very well because they're a couple of hard-hitting guys and they bring a lot of intensity to the ring. That's the big trademark of a

Shield match, that intensity, and that's what those guys bring in spades. We live for those moments where there's bruises and blood and teeth flying everywhere. The blood, sweat, and tears of the moment, where you're digging down twenty minutes into a match to bring out the best in each other — that's what all four of us are all about. There's an art to tag team wrestling. I love tag team wrestling. I'm really realizing how much I missed it. There's a big difference between six guys having a Six-Man Tag Team Match and four great tag team Superstars. When all four are great tag team Superstars and both are great teams, it really comes across in the match quality."

Not bad for a team who didn't even know if they'd make it past their first night. When The Shield first debuted in WWE back in November 2012 at *Survivor Series*, Ambrose says they were "thrown to the wolves. We were nobodies, and nobody in the business wanted to give us any help. It was a different time back then. They threw us right out into the deep end and we started swimming. We were like, 'Okay, you know what we're going to do? We're going to go out there and tear it up. We're going to work harder than everybody else every single night.' We really upped the pace of the whole company. Matches started getting faster, more stuff started happening, and there was an attitude shift when we came in. There were no nights off for us. There is a certain standard for a Shield match. Whether it's all three of us or just two of us. When me and Seth Rollins are defending the tag team titles on a pay-per-view, there's a certain standard that we hold ourselves to. We have to steal the show. We have to. And we all feel that together. When we're out there, we're constantly trying to prove to the whole world that The Shield is the best group of all time."

"We didn't have a theme song or an entrance," Rollins remembers. "We had turtlenecks and S.W.A.T. pants and that's about it. I think all three of us were all too concerned about just going out there and making an impression to worry about all that other stuff. For myself and Ambrose, we had been working on the independents for a long, long time before we had the opportunity to come to WWE and find

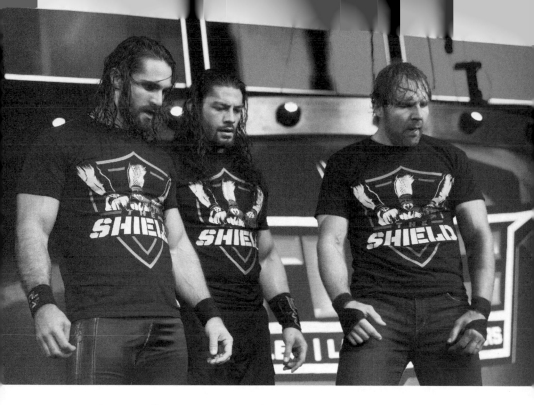

success here, so for us to get ourselves on WWE TV and on a WWE pay-per-view and to make such a huge impact, that was really special to us. And for Roman, he is someone who comes from a wrestling family, so he has heavy shoes to walk in. For him, he wanted to make an impression as well, so he didn't get left in the dust in his own family. So for all three of us, we were all just concerned about making an impact and making sure everything was done the right way, and, obviously, we'd figure out how to get out of turtlenecks and jeans and find something cooler the next day. We had no idea what our entrance music would be, but we figured we'd find out eventually. So it wasn't like, 'Here's your manufactured boy-band gimmick: this is exactly what it's going to look like, this is exactly what it's going to sound like, this is exactly what you're going to do.' We were given the freedom to make the most of our situation.

"We knew we were going to be in some sort of group, and initially it was a mixed bag. Some people thought we were going to be a security force for CM Punk, who at the time was in a story with Ryback and needed some backup. But in the end of the day, it turned into something

much more than that. After our debut in *Survivor Series* five years ago, people from within the company started to take notice and realize that we were going to be much more than just three flunkies for the champ at the time. It took on a life of its own after that, and it was up to us to create our own identities as a group and as individuals. So, honestly, the presentation of what The Shield was supposed to be never really happened; it was a grassroots thing that grew over time and turned into something much bigger than any of us ever expected it to be."

To Ambrose, there was never a time or match where he thought The Shield had finally made it. He felt constant pressure to prove the team belonged, not only on the show but at the top of the card. "The last five years have been such a whirlwind that it's hard to slow down and smell the roses," says Ambrose. "I'd say the moment that stands out is our very first match, inside the Barclays Center against three huge Superstars. They weren't setting us up for a gimme in our debut. I think someone got hurt and they shifted the card around, because they made the match very last minute. We didn't have much time to prepare for it. It was like, 'Okay, these three guys are good, here it is, a TLC Match. Let's do it.' We were just like, 'Fuck it.' We didn't care. It was cool. When we were coming down to the ring that night, it was very intense. Our careers, our lives could've all ended in this moment. Looking back, if we would've pooped the bed that night, our careers could've been over. It was hit a home run or strike out, and that's how your life is going to go. Looking back, it's funny to think about how things could've turned out if it went bad. At the time, we were so dead-set focused that nobody could mess with us. Afterward, we knew we had just arrived. Nobody could screw with us. But at the time, nobody realized the importance of what was happening. We were just making it up as we went along and trying to survive. We wanted to go out there and have the best match every show. We were just doing it.

"It was such an intense time because every single night we felt like our career was on the line. That's just the attitude we brought in. It was a very intense time," Ambrose continues. "We just thought The Shield was a means to an end. It was a way for us to get our foot in the door. We all had separate things we wanted to do. We all saw our futures in separate places. We didn't realize The Shield itself is what people were gravitating toward and was becoming so special to the WWE Universe. We didn't realize that until years later when everybody was calling for us to reunite. I've been away from them for longer than we were together, and I've had more success apart from them than I had together. But every single day we were apart, all I would hear was 'When is The Shield coming back?' It's something that stuck with people much more than we realized. When Seth and I started teaming together again, we could feel the energy, we could feel the way fans cared about us. We realize now in this second run how special and how much equity there is in The Shield."

But even with The Shield reunited, early rumors suggested the team wasn't going to be around long, with people (including the creative team behind the scenes) talking about plans for a Rollins versus Ambrose match at *WrestleMania* almost as soon as they won the Tag Team Championship. "I'm a big believer that everything happens for a reason, so I don't stress too much about the future," says Ambrose. "The nature of this business is that it changes every freakin' minute. You never know what's going to happen. I don't look any farther than a week ahead. I'm worried about today. You can prepare for the future, but you have to be able to change with the wind. Who knows what's coming. Seth and I have always had great chemistry in the ring, though. I never met Seth until I went to FCW. He always ran in different circles than I did. He was in Ring of Honor and places like that, and you'd find me in the more extreme scenarios. He was thrilling people with his athleticism while I was getting stabbed in the head with objects. We were on two different paths, but our parallel paths finally merged together in FCW. First time we ever wrestled as opponents, the chemistry and the mindset and the work ethic immediately clicked. The competitiveness was great, and the fact that we were always trying to one-up each other really brought our matches to another level. That's what makes us both such great partners . . . and opponents."

CHAPTER 9

Roode Awakening

AUGUST 22, 2017: *SMACKDOWN LIVE*

Two days after *SummerSlam*, *SmackDown LIVE* features the glorious debut of former NXT Champion (and 20-year vet) Bobby Roode. Roode is one step closer to fulfilling his lifelong dream of performing at *WrestleMania* — his match against Shinsuke Nakamura at *NXT TakeOver* the night before *WrestleMania 33* could be considered the best match of the entire weekend. "Shows how far NXT has come, that the match is even talked about like that," says Roode. "The interest it has not only with sports-entertainment fans across the world but also with the guys and girls inside the company is incredible. With NXT, the finger is always on the pulse, and there are always eyes on NXT and on the NXT Superstars because obviously these are the guys and girls who will be headed up to the main roster soon. A lot of the talent on the main roster want to work with these people, so they come to the shows to see what they're all about. Honestly, the NXT Universe is very, very passionate, and they're a little different than what you'd see during a *Monday Night Raw* or a *SmackDown LIVE* show. It's a very

different feel. It's a very passionate crowd. When it comes to *TakeOver*, there are only five matches on these shows, and every guy and girl on the card goes out there and tries to steal the show, and they're given a great amount of time to go out there and do their thing. It's always encouraging as a performer to look out in the crowd and see people from the main roster who have come to see what you do."

And to Roode, with all of those eyes on NXT, it's the perfect time to go out and try to steal not only the show but also the entire weekend away from the main roster. "That's the attitude for sure with NXT, for all of the *TakeOvers*," says Roode. "The *TakeOvers* are always the night before a major pay-per-view, whether it's *WrestleMania*, the *Royal Rumble*, *SummerSlam*, or *Survivor Series*, and the goal is always for *NXT TakeOver* to really push the main roster the next night and to outperform and have the best show of the weekend. And I'm sure that's their attitude now. There are a bunch of hard-working guys and girls down there who want to get to where I've gotten to now."

It was just a year earlier, at *NXT TakeOver: Dallas*, the night before *WrestleMania 32*, where Roode unexpectedly showed up and sat in the crowd, no contract in hand, but there was already interest on both sides. "I wasn't signed. I had a conversation with Triple H a few weeks earlier, getting a feel for what both of us were looking for. I told him what I wanted to do and what I wanted to be a part of, and at the end of the day, I really just wanted an opportunity. I had some experience, and I really felt like I had a good career up to that point, but I wanted the opportunity to come to WWE and show them what I had. I was given that opportunity and made the best of my situation and was put in a very good spot where I was able to perform in main events in NXT and work with some really great people.

"So at that point at *WrestleMania 32* in Dallas, I wasn't even signed. It was shortly thereafter where I signed the contract and got the working papers in order. One thing led to another and off we went. I was there as a guest. I was in the front row before Samoa Joe and Finn Bálor were in the main event, and the reaction I got from the NXT Universe gave me goosebumps. You really don't know how fans will react. Being in the business for twenty years, it doesn't mean a lot until you come to WWE and prove yourself. I got a pretty warm reception that night, so it was a really good feeling.

"The only opportunity to be a part of a *WrestleMania* is to be a part of this company, and honestly some feelers were sent out through some friends to see if we could make this happen," says Roode. "[NXT head trainer] Matt Bloom had a lot to do with that, as he put me on the phone with Triple H and we had a really good conversation. Things just went really quickly, and before you knew it, I was at *WrestleMania 32* in Dallas, and I was sitting in the front row at *NXT TakeOver*. I had a feeling of what WWE was about from the outside looking in, what the product was and how the company was viewed from a business perspective, but that weekend gave me the opportunity to see it from

the inside, to meet some pretty important people — from Triple H to some of the coaches down at NXT — and, most importantly, to get to know some of the talent and get a feel for how they were treated and what the company was all about. One thing led to another, and, quite quickly, I got my start right before *SummerSlam*. The rest is history.

"I wasn't sure how the WWE Universe and the NXT Universe would take to me when I debuted, so I was pretty nervous, but the response that I received was pretty overwhelming. The time that I had in NXT and the build to *WrestleMania* in Orlando put me in a position where I was walking in as a champion, facing Shinsuke Nakamura at the time. It was a really big deal for me. To accomplish what I accomplished in such a short amount of time in WWE and NXT — that was really special for me. To be in Orlando, that was home: that's where the Performance Center is; that's where NXT lives. So to perform at the Amway Center in a sold-out arena the night before *WrestleMania* was a pretty amazing experience."

Roode defeated the King of Strong Style in an incredible match that marked the end of Nakamura's reign in NXT while showcasing the Glorious One's hard-hitting, old-school style in the ring. Roode held the title for four months before dropping the Championship to Drew McIntyre at *NXT TakeOver: Brooklyn III*, and it was during that time period when Roode learned he was about to be fast-tracked to the main roster. "Triple H pulled me aside about a week before *TakeOver: Brooklyn III*," Roode explains. "He told me that the plan was to go up to *SmackDown*. He wasn't sure on the timing, if I was going up right away, or if they were going to hold me off for a bit, but I knew I was finishing up with NXT after *TakeOver: Brooklyn III* during *SummerSlam* weekend. And sure enough, there was the *SmackDown* the Tuesday after *SummerSlam*, and that's where I made my debut. Things moved quite quickly, and I'm very fortunate for that."

Roode also says he's fortunate for his theme song, "Glorious," a song that has taken on a life of its own since being introduced in NXT and has become a pop-culture phenomenon now that it has been introduced to a wider audience on *SmackDown*. "Honestly, it's been a blessing," says Roode. "The whole song and 'Glorious' gimmick is something I wasn't too sure of in the beginning, but obviously the song took off and had close to a million downloads on iTunes before I even made my debut. That was really cool, and now you see sports teams using it and people downloading it as ringtones and using it for weddings, so it has really taken on a life of its own. As a performer, when you have the opportunity to have a song like that and to have an entrance like I have, it definitely helps you. It helps you immensely, so I'm really grateful for that opportunity."

The popularity of the song helped elevate Roode with the creative team as they saw the response he got from day one on the *SmackDown* roster. Roode rocketed into the United States Championship scene while continuing his rivalry with Dolph Ziggler and Baron Corbin. Says Roode, "Dolph has always been one of those guys who I've watched, and I've always thought he was an amazing talent, so to walk in the door and to be put on the main roster and to work with Dolph immediately was a blessing. He's so talented, and he really helped me establish myself in front of the WWE Universe. It's a different crowd, it's a different feel each and every night compared to what I was used to in NXT. The NXT fans knew who I was when I walked in the door. I wasn't sure how the WWE Universe would react to me, but Dolph definitely helped me get over that point. My character was well liked in NXT, but my character on *SmackDown LIVE* is more of someone that people care for, and Dolph has made people care for me more by the way he comes across on television. But as far as the product, as far as the performances with Dolph, I couldn't ask for anything better."

With Roode's extensive wrestling background, the WWE Universe can also expect to see some matchups from his pre-WWE career, as Roode, Samoa Joe, and AJ Styles have all known each other for over a decade. "We knew we had what it took to be stars in this business; it was just about getting the right eyes on us," says Roode. "We bring a lot of experience, but, obviously, WWE is a different animal, and you have to perform at a certain level and jump over certain barriers, but I'd like to say that the three of us have adapted quite well and our success up to this point has proved that. It's a great feeling to be a part of WWE and to be a part of it with guys you've come up with."

Could the WWE Universe see one of those matchups at *WrestleMania* 34? "For me as a performer for the past nineteen, almost twenty years, I just try to take things one day at a time. When you get closer to that date, when you get closer to *WrestleMania*, you start to think about it more, but obviously I would love nothing more than to be a part of the show in a big way, and hopefully that happens. Hopefully I'm in a high-profile match, but you never know when opportunities will head your direction. I just need to make the best of my opportunities, just like I did in NXT."

CHAPTER 10
Flair for the Dramatic

SEPTEMBER 4, 2017: *MAE YOUNG CLASSIC*

When Stephanie McMahon, Triple H, Bayley, Alexa Bliss, and Asuka stood onstage at a business-partner summit and announced the *Mae Young Classic* back in April 2017, the 32-woman tournament was not only another step forward in the WWE Women's Evolution, it was a chance to bring in new talent from the independent scene to challenge the women of NXT. The tournament was shown over three nights, with the preliminary rounds taking place at NXT's home, Full Sail University, and the finals airing live on the WWE Network from Paradise, Nevada. And while the tournament final eventually crowns Kairi Sane the winner, the moment the WWE Universe is left talking about is the backstage confrontation between members of WWE's Four Horsewomen and the Ronda Rousey–led Four Horsewomen from MMA. Rousey alongside Marina Shafir and Jessamyn Duke are cheering on friend (and fellow Horsewoman) Shayna Baszler, who had made it to the tournament finals, when they run into Charlotte Flair, Bayley, and Becky Lynch, sparking a staredown and some trash talk,

with Rousey even saying, "You name the time, you name the place." As Flair, Bayley, and Lynch walk away, Rousey has the final word: "I'll be waiting for you." End scene.

It's a moment the WWE Universe has been waiting for since Rousey first proclaimed her love for WWE while reigning as the "baddest woman on the planet" in the UFC. She even showed up at *WrestleMania 31*, standing by The Rock's side before mixing it up against both Stephanie McMahon and Triple H. Was it finally time for Rousey to sign her WWE contract and join the roster full-time?

"It definitely has *WrestleMania* written all over it," says Flair when asked about a potential Four Horsewomen versus Four Horsewomen match. "With the four of us in NXT, it was, I hate to use this word, but it was so organic. The WWE Universe named us the Four Horsewomen. And I'm pretty sure that's what happened to them in MMA. Everyone knows what Ronda means to that sport as a whole, and she definitely opened the door for the women in WWE to show that women can main-event, women can make a difference, women can be the attraction. So to have that crossover and to have her take that interest in us just takes everything up to the next level. And then you add in the fact that I'm actually a Flair — I'm actually related to the original four — it just writes itself and is really cool. *WrestleMania* would be a perfect platform for this match.

"If it happens, I want this to be a big storyline. I would want weeks leading up to this where they're challenging us, we're challenging them. I don't know how it works, because Becky and I are on *SmackDown* and Sasha and Bayley are on *Raw*, but if we all came together on a pay-per-view, or if they weren't even announced that they were going to be there but something broke down where they interrupted a match or they called us out . . . I don't know. There's one thing to have it happen during the *Mae Young Classic* and for there to be buzz on *NXT*, but for it to happen in WWE on mainstream television, that's a whole different ballgame."

Flair thinks Rousey's athletic ability and popularity would lead to a great match, but for her to join the roster full-time, Flair believes the UFC star would first need heavy training in NXT. "When you think Ronda Rousey, you think badass, so she doesn't need to develop her character in front of the WWE Universe, she already has it, she's already a superstar, so she can come into *WrestleMania* as is, no problem," she says. "But to be a WWE Superstar full-time, she definitely has to have more training, but she has the type of crossover star power where she can just show up and say, 'Hey, I'm here,' and the fans would love to see it. The equivalent would be Mayweather versus Conor McGregor. Whether or not anybody thought McGregor had a chance, it was everything he brings to the table and what he represents and his confidence and his character . . . it didn't matter that it was boxing and not MMA, it was how they built the fight around the characters. The story alone sold the fight, and that's what they can do in WWE with the Four versus Four. We can see what they stand for, what they represent, and they would enter a different ring,

but it would be really exciting for everyone. Once we get a Four versus Four faceoff on *Raw* or *SmackDown* or a pay-per-view, it's all eyes on. It will be interesting to see what Ronda is going to do. Where her career is at right now and how she just got married, as much as it would do for us, it would be exciting for her career as well."

And if the Four Horsewomen versus Four Horsewomen isn't booked, Flair hopes to earn a one-on-one shot against Rousey. "That's my goal, I just don't want to be a WWE Superstar, I want to be an attraction for the company as a female," she says. "Brock Lesnar, an attraction. John Cena, an attraction. Roman Reigns, an attraction. I want to represent that as a female, and to be able to face her in a one-on-one match would prove that I have that kind of star power, that I can be an attraction. I'm known for my talent, not my looks — not that it's not like that across the board — so that would be a dream to have Charlotte Flair verses Ronda Rousey headlining. Even if it's Four versus Four and it breaks down into that, it would be unbelievable."

Could a Four Horsewomen versus Four Horsewomen or Charlotte Flair versus Ronda Rousey end up as the co–main event? That's a question that wouldn't have even been considered just a few years ago, but after the Divas Revolution turned into the Women's Evolution and the WWE Universe became heavily invested in Superstars like Charlotte Flair, Sasha Banks, and Alexa Bliss, the notion of a women's match as the main attraction to WWE's supershow no longer seems so far-fetched. "It's come a long way," says Flair. "For one, we went from Divas to Superstars. If you were a fan walking into *WrestleMania* 32 at AT&T Stadium, you saw myself, Becky, and Sasha in the center of that poster alongside legends like Undertaker and Triple H. You had Shane McMahon and Roman Reigns, but with us in the center, it was the men who looked like the eye candy. When you walked up, it was like, wow, these three girls are the main attraction of the largest *WrestleMania* we've had to date: 101,000 people. Now that's a statement. The attraction just happened to be three girls. *Total Divas* has also opened doors to new viewers and a new audience to see what it's like for the women, but when they retired the Divas

Championship and gave the women a brand new title, it was refreshing, saying, 'Hey, we're updating the product, we're giving the women a new platform, we went from Divas to Women, and now the title looks like the men's title. I think that's also a reflection of how they feel about us. I was honored to be the last Divas Champion and to retire the Divas Championship because there was so much history, but when they gave us that new title, they were saying this is the new era. And now there are multiple women's matches, and we've gone from main-eventing *Raw* and *SmackDown* to main-eventing *Hell in a Cell* to being inside the cage at *Starrcade* to the Ladder Match . . . giving us all the same opporrnties as the men. Now, no matter if it's male or female, you know you're going to get a great show versus thinking, 'Oh, it's just the women.'

"The change all started when Triple H hired Sara Del Rey as the first female coach. They turned FCW into NXT, and we revamped the entire developmental program into something that now isn't even developmental, it's really the third brand. And I think when NXT started having those *TakeOvers* and the women started stealing the show and had just as many fans come to see them and had just as much support as the male matches, Triple H didn't second-guess the women, he just said, 'Hey, this is the story, this is the match, this is what we're going with.' And then it led to what it is today and it has just worked its way up to the main roster. Hunter made the executive decision to hire Sara Del Rey, who is known and respected and has done every type of wrestling all over the world from Japan to Mexico. It was Hunter who realized that the women needed a woman to represent them in the ring and to represent them in the meetings."

These days, Flair and the rest of the Horsewomen know that to stay on top, they need to keep pushing the envelope. "You never get complacent and you stay hungry," says Flair. "We had the Triple Threat at *WrestleMania 32*, we had the 4-Way last year, me and Sasha main-evented *Raw*, we main-evented *SmackDown*, we main-evented a pay-per-view, but we know that we can do more. I feel like I've only scratched the surface. One day soon, we will be in that main event at *WrestleMania*."

CHAPTER 11
Headbutt Heard 'Round the World

SEPTEMBER 12, 2017: *SMACKDOWN LIVE*

All year, Kevin Owens's rivalry with the McMahon family has been heating up. After losing the United States Championship to AJ Styles in a Triple Threat Match that saw Styles pin Chris Jericho and not the defending champ, Owens demanded a rematch. But after Styles defeated Owens at *SummerSlam*, Owens blamed special referee Shane McMahon for the loss, demanding another rematch, only this time with a competent referee. Shane agreed, giving Owens his choice of ref, but his choice, Baron Corbin, walked out mid-match, leaving Shane once again to fill the void. Styles defeated Owens, but the cocky villain again blamed Shane for the loss. The following week on *SmackDown*, Owens verbally assaulted Shane, even insulting his kids, which caused *SmackDown*'s Commissioner to attack the big man. The result? General Manager Daniel Bryan announced Shane's suspension and Owens was visited by Vince McMahon on the following week's episode. On September 12, the Chairman strutted to the ring and announced Kevin Owens would face his son, Shane, inside Hell in a Cell at the upcoming

Hell in a Cell pay-per-view. Owens was livid, shaking Vince's hand, but as the two jawed at each other, Owens stepped in, ferociously head-butting his 72-year-old boss and busting him open. With McMahon left bloodied on the ground, Owens had just pulled off one of the most shocking moments of 2017.

"It's always crazy to be in the ring with guys you've watched your whole life," says Owens. "Vince McMahon pretty much shaped my childhood, and he's shaping my adulthood and my entire life at this point, through his creation. So to be in the ring with him and to get to do anything with Vince McMahon is always a big deal.

"When we were in the ring, he was talking a lot of shit. He was getting me riled up, he was riled up, and when we were ready to go, I didn't think about how hard I was going to hit him, I just hit him like I would anybody else. I just let it fly."

And while most suspect this moment will eventually lead Owens to face McMahon's son-in-law, Triple H, at *WrestleMania*, Owens is hoping for something a bit different.

"After doing what we did in the ring, I couldn't help but start thinking about Vince McMahon having one last match at *WrestleMania* — against myself, fingers crossed," says Owens. "When anybody asks me about dream matches for *WrestleMania*, Triple H is at the top of the list, but there's something about being in the ring against Vince McMahon at *WrestleMania* that's just so unfathomable. If that became a possibility, that's the match I would want. If me against Triple H doesn't happen this year, it can happen next year, it can happen the year after that. Triple H still has a lot of good years left in him. But who knows how many matches Vince McMahon has left, or even if he's got one left in him at all. But if he does have one, it has got to be at *WrestleMania*, and I think, right now, I'm the guy who he should be in a match with."

But first, Owens has to deal with the younger McMahon at *Hell in a Cell*. The two battled up and down the cage, with Owens hitting a pop-up powerbomb on top of the cell's roof, before the fight led to McMahon setting up for his patented Leap of Faith elbow-drop from

the top of the cage. As McMahon flew down toward Owens, Sami Zayn appeared, yanking Owens out of the way just in time, causing McMahon to smash through the table. Zayn pushed Owens on top for the pin, giving Kevin the victory, while giving Zayn the biggest spotlight (and turn) in his WWE career.

Owens still can't get the moment of Shane hurtling his body toward him out of his mind, as the timing of the stunt had to be perfect or Owens, Zayn, and McMahon could've all been seriously injured. And because of the nature of the fall, Shane's dive could not be practiced beforehand, with Zayn only being told to grab Owens once he saw McMahon's feet leave the cell. "I felt more than the wind as he flew past me, I think I felt him actually touch me," says Owens. "But thankfully I was out of Dodge just in time. It's pretty scary to know that he could land on you, but Sami pulled me away just in time and we avoided disaster for ourselves. It didn't work out so hot for Shane, but, obviously, he's very tough, and he bounced back to TV pretty quickly. I'm sure that's going to lead to some more interesting moments between all of us.

"Being in Hell in a Cell, no matter who it's against, is really cool. It's such an iconic structure within WWE. Being in the ring with Shane — again, you're in the ring with someone you watched growing up. It's Shane McMahon. Besides Stephanie and Triple H, there's nobody higher ranked in the company than Shane McMahon. I've said this about so many matches and so many opponents I've had in WWE, but the Hell in a Cell Match is something I'll never forget. I don't know anybody who would climb to the top and not be intimidated when they look down. You can't tell how high it is when you're standing on the ground looking up. You know it's big, you know it's high, but once you get up there, it's really wild to look around and look down at all the people. When I was standing up there, I was looking around the arena, and I was eye level with people who were in the thirtieth row of the bleachers. It was crazy, and it's all part of a really incredible experience. It's hard to put into words for somebody who has never gone through something like that, that's for sure."

Besides the match itself, Owens was also excited to work alongside Zayn. The two have been heated rivals for years, with their NXT friction spilling over to the main roster, but in reality, Owens and Zayn both describe their relationship more like brothers. "We've known each other for fifteen years," says Owens, recalling their years on the independent scene together. "We've been all over the world together. We've experienced so much together, and I call him my brother and he calls me his brother and that's what we are; we're best friends. We don't always like each other, but we'll always have a special bond after everything that we've been through. It's great to be able to work together and show a different side of ourselves. It has really been a lot of fun so far.

"Sami's one of the many who deserves a break and a chance to show what he can do on a bigger stage. I'm glad he got his opening now. There are a lot of guys like him who are very good and who people might not realize who they are, but I'm sure they'll all eventually get their opportunity, and I'm glad to see him get his."

This is the second time in recent memory where an Owens "friendship" has driven his storyline, as his tour with Chris Jericho was one of the most captivating storylines heading into *WrestleMania 33*. "My favorite moment was the *Festival of Friendship* when I turned on him. It was very special, very well done, and there were a lot of moments throughout the story that were just a lot of fun," says Owens. "The payoff was me turning on him and us having the match at *WrestleMania*. I wish the match at *WrestleMania* had gone a bit differently, honestly, but everything leading up to the match was very fun."

As for how Owens keeps ending up in the spotlight when other talent seem to rise and fall within the WWE hierarchy, Owens attributes it to his drive and passion for the business. "That's not a knock on anybody else, and I'm not implying that other people aren't as passionate or as driven as I am, but the difference is that I'll take no for an answer because once in a while, you have to," explains Owens. "But I'll pitch ideas, I'll try to come up with ideas, I'll talk to people, and I'm constantly trying to be relevant. To me, there's nothing worse than not being relevant. I'm not saying I'm always going to be in the top angle or the top story, that's just not realistic, but I want to feel like what I'm doing matters. Maybe it's just a matter of time. Maybe once you're here for ten years, you just start to enjoy the ride and you don't care so much about whether or not you're featured prominently, but I've never been that way. I've been doing this for seventeen years — I was doing this for fifteen years before WWE — and I've been all around the world, and I've never been happy with being complacent, even if I had been with a company for seven years. I always try to keep myself relevant and make sure that what I'm doing means something. It's just a byproduct of that kind of attitude, I'd say."

Now all Owens wants is for that passion to pay off, to turn that tireless drive into a match against Vince McMahon at *WrestleMania 34*.

Says Owens, "I'm not looking to be the best match, I'm not looking to be the best, I'm not looking for people to look at me and think that I am the best in the world. I don't care. I want people to look at me and remember what I did and have memorable moments from my match. I want them to walk away and talk about what I did, whether it's a moment or part of the match or an actual match, I want to leave them with memories. I've always been about that, whether it's *WrestleMania* or not. At *WrestleMania*, that touch is multiplied. That's what it's all about. It's about creating memories that will last a lifetime."

CHAPTER 12

Welcome to The
Uso Penitentiary

OCTOBER 8, 2017: *HELL IN A CELL*

How do you end a classic storyline that saw The Usos and The New Day rock *SummerSlam* while helping define the current tag team era? Kendo sticks, and lots of them. It was the first-ever Tag Team Championship Match held inside the Hell in a Cell cage, and the two teams put together some of the most innovative (and violent) offense the WWE Universe has ever witnessed. The match involved handcuffs; Big E hitting a running spear through the ropes and flying headfirst into the cage; Woods using the kendo sticks to trap one of the Usos against the cage in his own prison; and a flurry of vicious double-team kendo stick shots by The Usos against a hanging Woods unlike anything seen before inside a WWE ring.

"The most fun part about our job is trying to put something like that together," says Jey Uso. "We're playmakers, all you need is the right dance partner. You need someone who will know all the steps, and when you pop that thing out and you go out there and you execute it, you can hear the reaction, and you know instantly you have something special. You know, okay, when we hit this, the crowd should be at this level, and when we follow that up, they should be at the next level, and you're building the match so the crowd is always going up-up-up. It was a cakewalk with The New Day. I'm not going to lie, not all matches are that easy. Some matches are hard. We had four matches out of the Top 25 on WWE.com, so you know it was more than chemistry — we had the whole scientific lab up in there."

"We didn't even go back and watch any of that history of *Hell in a Cell* — that just wasn't in our mindset," adds Jimmy. "We didn't go back and watch all of the old matches to try to get ideas. When we got together with The New Day, ideas were just flowing. We laid it out, it sounded good, it looked good on paper, and when we went out there and executed — you're seeing something come to life and it's cool, and the people were into it, and we were into it, and you just can't get that feeling nowhere else in the world other than Hell in a Cell, and we had that feeling. You can't explain that."

What they can explain is the Bryce Harper–like swings each of the brothers took with the kendo sticks, striking Woods again and again and again in one of the most painful and cringe-inducing moments of WWE TV in 2017. "When we were kids, we used to love playing baseball," laughs Jimmy. "Jey struck out all the time. I had way more home runs than he had. Me and Roman would hit the ball, Jimmy would swing hard, but he wasn't making too much contact. He was making contact that night, though."

"I wasn't holding back," adds Jey. "And in those kind of matches, you cannot hold back and neither can they. When you hold back, the crowd can see it, and when they see you holding back, you just buried everyone in the ring."

To Woods, it's just part of the program and something he actually called for. "Horrible. It was really horrible, but I knew it was going to be bad when I threw the idea in the hat," he says. "For me, I wanted to tell a couple of different stories in that match. It's a full-on, drag-out fight in the beginning, then it turns into me just getting obliterated,

and I'm seen as more of E's little brother. Then by the end of it, I come back from the grave, essentially, to try and help E. I realize in the match that yeah, I'm the little brother of this group, and I might not win this fight, but you're not going to win unless you put me down. I think that came across in the match, and we were all able to elevate the match and continue to do more stuff — stuff you've never seen before — and I think people in the crowd really respect that. We put so much time and effort into delivering at the show; we're not just going out there and doing the same thing every time. We're actually taking the time to work together and think of new stuff, trying to deliver a match and moments within the match that people will remember.

"The WWE Universe might not realize how much that kendo stick hurts. It feels terrible. It's not good at all. People know what we do, they understand that it's entertainment, but things get a little more intense than people realize. They know it's entertainment when they buy the ticket, but we add a crux of realism in there so people will feel for us, feel for The New Day a little bit more because we're being strung up and beat with kendo sticks. After the first shot, everybody in the crowd is like, 'Oh man, that sucks,' but then it turns into them teeing off on me. I told them not to let up, I told them that no matter how I'm screaming or what I'm screaming, just keep going, I don't care if it's too much. We'll talk about that a few days later. By the time they stopped swinging those kendo sticks, there was a different feeling in the crowd. Everyone was like, 'This is gross, they need to stop, I feel bad for Mr. Woods.' Which translates into 'I feel bad for The New Day,' so they want to see us break out of those handcuffs, come back, and beat the crap out of The Usos. The violence level is something that, every now and then, we take advantage of, and I have the scars on my body and all over my stomach to keep that reminder fresh in my head."

To The Usos, being a part of *Hell in a Cell* was about more than just wowing the WWE Universe and brutalizing Xavier Woods, it was about history, as they are following in the footsteps of their father, WWE Hall of Famer Rikishi. Back in 2000, at the *Armageddon* pay-per-view, Undertaker famously chokeslammed Rikishi off the Hell in a Cell roof and onto a truck bed packed with pine chips in one of the most dangerous stunts of the Attitude Era. "Man, it just hypes us up," says Jey. "This is part of history now. Look at it. Our pops was in there with Taker and Rock, and Undertaker chokeslammed him off Hell in a Cell, and now here we are, the first tag team title match ever in Hell in a Cell. We're making our own footprints in the sand."

"And you feel it, like when we stepped in the cage, that was our first time ever being in Hell in a Cell, and when we stepped in there, you actually feel the vibe," says Jimmy. "It was really dope because we heard our fans give us respect, and everybody on social media was saying that Hell in a Cell actually looked like the Uso Penitentiary after that match. It wasn't Hell in a Cell, we were in the Uso Penitentiary for that split second. It was cool stepping in there, and it's amazing being part of that history now."

"Growing up watching wrestling, it was normal to us: 'Hey, Pops is on TV,'" adds Jey. "We knew we could watch him and we'd watch everybody, from The Tonga Kid to Jimmy Snuka to Yokozuna. It was just a natural thing. It's hard to explain, but it's like your dad going to work and clocking in; only thing is, our dad was clocking in to *Monday Night Raw*. We didn't even think about becoming wrestlers, though, because growing up our thing was football. My dad loved us playing football. He always told us education and sports first, wrestling will always be there to fall back on. We wanted to try some stuff, and, while football didn't work out, I'm glad we're here. I'm glad we made that move."

A move that their father had warned them about, offering some advice that has stuck with the brothers. "My dad has been in this game for over twenty years, and he told us, 'This is a game full of sharks, so watch each other's backs,'" says Jey. "And it took us a while to get it, but we get it now. My dad went up and down this road by himself, but at least we have each other to do all these miles and early flights and rental cars with. We get to do that struggle together. Plus we always have road partners: me, my brother, and his wife, Trinity [Naomi]. We got a good road crew, and that's the key to this. You gotta have a good road crew."

"We're still having fun," adds Jimmy. "We're away from our family and our kids, but at least when we're out here, we still have that feeling, it's still fun to us. When we go to Gorilla, right before we walk through that curtain, we're still nervous. We still come out here and we still get that funny feeling, that hasn't gone away yet. When that feeling goes away, that's the time to call it. But having fun, that's the main thing. When we come to work, it doesn't feel like work. We have fun for those fifteen minutes, those thirty minutes we're in the ring. The work starts when we're driving four hours or catching a flight or waiting in line to get the rental car.

"But to us, we grew up watching tag teams, so we're proud of the team we are, the team we're becoming. We grew up watching The Hart Foundation, we grew up watching the Legion of Doom, the Samoan Swat Team, and our family did tag team wrestling, so when we grew up, it was already a part of us. And us being twins, everything we go through, everything we've been through, we've done it together. When we came into WWE, the tag team division is all we had, so we knew we had to hit it hard, and now we see teams like Cesaro and Sheamus killing it. Dean and Seth were killing it before Dean got hurt. New Day is killing it. Breezango is on the rise. There are a lot of tag teams out here who might not have been given the opportunity yet, but once me and my brother got ours, once they gave us the stick and allowed us to open up and be ourselves, we made the best of our opportunity, and we're still growing. I can't wait to see where we'll be in another year, and then another year after that, but tag team wrestling is as hot as it has ever been, and we're making it 'hard to follow.' Too bad that phrase was on AJ's shirt first, but it's a real thing."

CHAPTER 13
Creative Control

OCTOBER 9, 2017: WWE HEADQUARTERS,
STAMFORD, CONNECTICUT

Six months to *WrestleMania 34*, and the only match penciled in is Roman Reigns versus Brock Lesnar. This is in stark contrast to how WWE Creative worked in the past, as writers would plot what they thought would make up the best *WrestleMania* card a year in advance, then book the storylines backward to lead their way up to the big show. "I'm sure the closer we get to it, questions will be raised: 'What's Undertaker's availability? Is that on the table? Where do we go with Braun?' Outside of Roman and Brock, which is a match we've been building up to for two years now, nothing is set in stone," says Ed Koskey, WWE's Vice President of Creative Writing, who started as a Production Assistant back in 2001 and now is one of the most influential writers behind the scenes at the Stamford office. "It's one of those deals where we'll see where everything lays out. Last year, we knew we were going to get Jericho and Owens, we knew we were doing Seth and Hunter. Some years you have more lined up, and other years you're just waiting to see how stuff pans out. That's just where we're at.

"In the course of a year, so much stuff can happen, with injuries being the most serious situation. If someone gets hurt, we are forced to change plans, then just when you think you have something set, someone else might go down, and everything changes again. We knew where we were going for this year's *WrestleMania* main event two years ago, but that could change at the drop of a hat. Because of the amount of content we do on a weekly and monthly basis, we just can't lay things out as far in advance as we used to. Now you go to John Cena versus Roman Reigns in September instead of saving it until *WrestleMania*. You're trying to get these talents over, but there are different success stories and different stories of failure. You pitch something and you think, 'Yes, this is going to happen, it's going to be great,' but then it just doesn't work out. Or you have someone like Braun Strowman last year. He was on a roll, but he didn't have a prominent place in *WrestleMania*. So we said, 'Let's put him in the Andre the Giant Battle Royal,' and he'd probably win that, but in the course of pitching that and the time of the show, Gronk became available, so guess what, he's not winning the battle royal anymore. The spot went to Mojo Rawley, and it turns out Braun didn't need that spotlight to maintain his roll, you just need to keep building him up the night after and you keep going. You still have a star on your hands with Braun; the story just didn't work out the way we anticipated. I'm sure he was pissed. We tried to shine the battle royal up a little bit by putting Andre the Giant's name on it to make it feel special, but there's always a handful of guys who want to be doing something else than just being in the battle royal."

To come up with the storylines, the creative team of about 25 people are split up to work on different aspects and different shows. "There's a group that stays back in the offices so they can keep working and get out ahead of the weekly shows. Then there is a team that goes out on the road and goes to the pay-per-views and weekly TV, then come back to the office on Thursdays," explains Koskey. "That's the one day a week where the entire team is under one roof. The road team goes to both shows, so there isn't a delineation between *Raw* and *SmackDown*, but the home teams, they are a little more split up: we have a group working on *Raw*, for both the television show and the pay-per-view coming up, then there is a team working on everything *SmackDown* for the next month. That way, when the road team comes back, we can hit the ground running, since the home team has already been working on various plans. The way the process used to work, everybody was doing everything. The whole team would go on the road, then we'd come back on a Wednesday after two days of travel, but you couldn't see straight, and you were tired, so you'd end up putting shows together over the weekends, then you'd hit the road again and start the process all over. Back then, everybody was trying to churn things out seven days a week, but it was just so tough, from both a personal and a professional standpoint. Everybody was just burnt out and you weren't able to give it your best all the time. Now, everything is more regimented and a little more structured, and people can carry the burden of the workload a little better, especially now when we're also helping with *NXT*. Divvying up the work has really been beneficial."

In terms of the writing team members, Vince McMahon acts as the

Lead Writer. Triple H acts as the Executive Vice President of Talent and Creative, with Koskey, Dave Kapoor, and Brian James (aka Road Dogg) leading the team of writers and reporting to Vince directly. The writing team comes from various backgrounds, ranging from former in-ring performers to Hollywood script writers. Says Koskey, "Brian James brings that in-ring perspective. Michael Hayes [WWE Hall of Famer and former Freebird] is still very much a part of the creative process. For the rest of us, we have various writing and TV backgrounds. Some come from a TV news perspective, a lot come from a Hollywood writing perspective, and some come in out of college as writers' assistants, taking notes. These are our grinders, learning the system from the ground up, then they graduate on to become writers. Some people come in as huge fans and have a deep knowledge of WWE's history; others come in and are new to us but, once they got the opportunity, became very much into it.

"In the end, though, it's still Vince running the show creatively, and he will until he's no longer with us," says Koskey. "There's been different attempts to put different people in charge. Stephanie McMahon was in charge for a while but transferred over to other opportunities with branding. Vince has the final say over everything. Anything you see on TV happens because Vince approved it to happen, so it only makes sense to give us direct access to Vince in order to pitch stories and get stuff approved and move forward."

And Vince doesn't care if it's his lead writer, a Superstar, or a guy in marketing who comes up with the idea, as long as it's a good idea. "One of the things we try to teach is you have to be careful about pride of authorship or digging in on a certain guy who you think has to be in the storyline," says Koskey. "The blessing and the curse of working for Vince is, in his mind, the best idea wins. He doesn't care if it comes from one of the writers over the process of a formal meeting, or if it comes from the janitor while he's drinking a cup of coffee. If the janitor says, 'Hey, how about this?' and it's a great idea, Vince will use it. When we're in production meetings and we have some of the guys who have backgrounds in the ring like Jamie Noble, Arn Anderson, and Mike Rotunda, they'll come in with their own suggestions, like, 'I like what you're doing here, but how about this?' Vince has been known to say, 'You're right, this is the way to go,' and he'll change the story on the spot. You can't get too wed to an idea where it has to be a certain way or it won't work at all. You can express how strongly you want something and do it in your most professional way possible, but, ultimately, once Vince makes his decision, then it's our job to get on the same side of the rope and start pulling it the same direction. You can't mope or drag your feet or feel like it should be this guy instead of that guy — you made your case, the judge heard it, but he ruled the other way."

As for the internet rumors of Vince never sleeping and calling meetings at 3 a.m. to go over storylines, Koskey simply laughs and calls it all urban legend. "Vince is always available. You can always call him or text him, but Vince doesn't call at three in the morning on some random Friday like, 'What if we do this with John Cena.' Doesn't happen," he says. "Sometimes when we're all traveling and it's after a show and everybody is up, you might get a phone call from Vince, like, 'I looked over the show for tomorrow, and I think this or that needs to change,' and it might be 2:30 in the morning, but that's because that's when everybody just got in from the show."

When pitching stories and which Superstars to push, Koskey said Vince is always listening to the crowd, while also taking into account live-event ticket and merchandise sales: what's working, what isn't working, what people are buying, what people aren't buying, and who they are paying to see. "Roman Reigns sells tickets," Koskey says, defending the company's top star. "Even though guys may boo him, others may cheer him, either way, when he comes out, it's loud in the arena and that's cool with us. He's a star and people want to see him, whether they want to boo or to cheer, to see him win or to see him lose, they are there for him. He's a star and he moves the needle. Roman is a second-generation guy, and he just looks the part. He looks like he was created in Vince's lab. He's everything you want a Superstar to be: he has that charisma, that star power, and that star factor.

"People react to him. People are drawn to him, whether they are saying 'Roman sucks!' or 'Let's go, Roman!' With the advent of social media, everybody wants to choose a side. It makes it fun. It's not like the old days where everybody in the stands loved Stone Cold Steve Austin. That's a unicorn. These days, you ride with the guy the audience is having fun with, that's all that matters. As long as they're having fun and making noise, it's all good."

The most important factor in WWE's creative success is the writing team working together to help shape Vince's vision, not what particular Superstar stands at the top of the card. "When Vince picks a direction and everybody gets behind it, we can do great things," says Koskey. "When *Great Balls of Fire* happened, that was supposed to be Braun versus Brock, but then Braun injured his elbow, so we thought he wasn't going to make the pay-per-view. At that point, we didn't know who was going to get that shot. But then Samoa Joe stepped up. Physically, he looks the part, he could be a match for Brock Lesnar. So Vince said, 'Hey, the next five weeks after *Extreme Rules* are all about making the wider audience familiar with Samoa Joe's history as a badass in the business. It's all about making him as badass and as much of a threat to Brock as possible.' So for those five weeks, that's what we did, and it paid off with a successful *Great Balls of Fire*, and then that led to Joe being added to *SummerSlam*. When Vince tells us, 'Get everyone on board, this is who we're going with,' you give that guy opportunities and do everything you can to make it work, and that's usually when we do our best work. You can usually only do that with one guy at a time, though, because of how the rosters are set up. With the amount of content we have to fill, it's tough to give the kind of push to more than one guy at a time. Sometimes you're just trying to find as many compelling things as you can for a three-hour show or a two-hour show every week. That's where you run into 'Well, let's not use this guy to get that guy over because this guy is pretty valuable.

Let's use him for this instead.' You're trying to serve a lot of masters and that's where you get into the fifty-fifty booking, where a guy who loses this week wins the next week so his reputation isn't hurt too bad. It's just not as great as when we say, 'This is the guy!' and we put our full force behind that push."

For now, Roman is that guy, but Koskey and crew are still trying to piece together the rest of the *WrestleMania 34* card, all the while knowing that changes can happen up until show time. "At *WrestleMania 33*, Dean Ambrose and Baron Corbin got shifted to the pre-show, where initially they weren't," he explains. "Again, it's one of those deals where we try to look at things with fresh eyes. So you might think this is what we're doing, but as you get closer to the show, you start thinking what if we did it this way. That's one of the fun parts of the job. You might wake up one morning and think you have everything set, but then someone comes in and says, 'What about this?' And it's a better idea, so then you have to change things and shuffle everything around. Sometimes it can change the day before. Usually, the day of *WrestleMania* we're pretty much set. The production meeting of *WrestleMania* takes place on the Friday before the show, and that's really the last moment where everybody is in the room together, looking at how the show lays out and giving their thoughts on the order and any other outstanding issues that might pop up. That's where stuff can change. Usually on game day, things are pretty much set, unless when guys are talking through their match they realize they need more time, that can change things, but for the most part everything is decided by the time we get to *WrestleMania* Sunday.

"Then again, you never know what could happen or if Vince will change his mind. The famous story would be Taker versus Brock. Vince went back and forth in his mind a bunch of times about whether or not to end Undertaker's *WrestleMania* undefeated streak. Vince went back and forth, back and forth, until eventually he decided to have Brock go over, and he didn't decide that until the day of *Mania*. But that's a once-in-a-lifetime choice. Winners and losers for everything else — that's already decided before we even travel to the show. At that point, we're already looking past *WrestleMania* and starting to think about what comes next. Now the *Raw* the night after *WrestleMania* almost has as high of expectations as *WrestleMania* itself. The seven-hour *WrestleMania* was pretty good, but what are they doing the next night? Who is coming out? Who is the surprise? Who is the return? What are they going to do to top it? How many beach balls will be in the crowd?

"It usually gets to the point where I send the final script out for *WrestleMania*, and I'm already working on Monday night's show. It's never over. We joke that the time from when *WrestleMania* ends to the time of the production meeting for *Raw* the next night is the off-season, hope you enjoyed it. The new season begins tonight. After *WrestleMania*, we can go to the after party and grab a drink, but then you realize, oh my goodness, we have a lot of work to do before tomorrow. Other times you realize, we're in pretty good shape, so you can grab a cocktail and toast the night before getting ready for *Raw*."

CHAPTER 14
They Don't Want None

NOVEMBER 19, 2017: *SURVIVOR SERIES*

Take a look at the best matches of 2017, and there's one undeniable (some would say phenomenal) constant. AJ Styles versus John Cena at *Royal Rumble*. AJ Styles versus Shane McMahon at *WrestleMania 33*. AJ Styles versus Kevin Owens versus Chris Jericho for the United States Championship on *SmackDown LIVE*. AJ Styles versus Finn Bálor at *TLC*. AJ Styles versus Brock Lesnar at *Survivor Series*. All of these thrilling matches capture the drama, intensity, and showmanship the WWE Universe craves, and the one man laying it all on the line in each of these Superstar slugfests is the high-flying phenom, AJ Styles.

Fans and fellow Superstars alike refer to Styles as "The Best in the World," and with the amount of high-quality, high-impact matches he adds to his resume on a monthly basis, it's easy to see why. But when AJ Styles left New Japan Pro Wrestling and was negotiating to join WWE, he wasn't sure if the deal was even going to take place, as he had attempted to make the jump years earlier, but WWE didn't sign him. "It was just timing. Timing is everything," said Styles. "It wasn't about me coming, it was about whether or not WWE wanted me. At the time, I knew Shinsuke Nakamura was leaving. He didn't know I knew, but I knew, and I thought, 'Wow, this is going to be a big blow to New Japan.' So I thought let me see what I can do to take steps in the right direction, maybe in America. Not necessarily WWE, because I tried to coordinate with them before, but they didn't have any interest.

"What happened this time, though, is there were a lot of guys hurt. A lot of big stars in WWE were injured at the time, and they needed someone who could come in and fill the mid-card, maybe the upper mid-card. I think that's what they had in mind when I came over. That's why they even wanted me in the first place, because I was a guy who could step right into the mid-card. I don't think they knew what I was capable of, or maybe they did, but they knew Vince McMahon wasn't excited about the guy he saw in the ring, at least, for a moment. Things changed pretty quickly, though, and WWE put a lot of faith in me, and things worked out the way they should. It was just all about timing."

The timing worked out perfectly for Styles as he made his debut in the 2016 *Royal Rumble* at the Amway Center in Orlando, Florida, an event where Styles was greeted by the WWE Universe with roars of delight. "Still gives me goosebumps," said Styles, who began wrestling professionally back in 1998 but calls the *Rumble* the single greatest night of his career. "Oh my God. That's the moment in my wrestling career that I will never forget. My biggest moment by far. I was worried that I had been out of the country for a while and maybe people don't care about AJ Styles. Does the WWE Universe even know who AJ Styles is? There were a lot of questions in my mind, and first impressions are everything. When you're in WWE, WWE is everything, and there is this bubble that you're in. I know Vince McMahon is in this bubble, and his only concern is what he's doing and how he can make it better. So you have no time to watch anything else. I knew Vince McMahon did not even know who I was as I understood it, but I knew Road Dogg and a couple of the other guys from before I was in WWE. They knew what I was capable of, but I don't think anybody could've imagined the response I got when I walked

through the curtain, when "Phenomenal" popped up on the Titan Tron and the crowd went absolutely nuts. It was just magic. It was the greatest moment in my career without a doubt."

But even after his wild reception at the *Rumble*, Styles says that it wasn't until a few months later that Vince McMahon started to appreciate everything "The Phenomenal One" could do. "There was a point where Vince said, 'I've seen you as the babyface, but I need you to be a bulldog.' He wanted to see a pit bull, those were his words. I was like I can be that guy, I know that guy. That's who I was when I wrestled in high school and college, I just went and hurt everybody. That's the way I wrestled, that's the way I played football. I didn't tackle guys to tackle them: I hit them so they didn't want to play anymore. And wrestling was the same way. I was trying to win the match before we even stepped on the mat. My opponents were so frightened that I was going to hurt them. Of course, I would keep it in the legal boundaries of what we were doing, but it was going to be rough. So I knew who Vince wanted, because that's who I was anyway. When I showed that aggression, that's when it changed everything for Vince. He was like whoa, and for a guy my size, I know I have to be able to show something else, and I showed him I have that aggressive side to me, and I think that's when everything changed."

And that trust paid off with championship runs, an ongoing rivalry against John Cena, and even a *WrestleMania* match against Shane McMahon, a match that was critically panned heading into the event but ended up being (what else?) the match of the night. "Going into *WrestleMania*, I thought Shane and I had a good story, but I don't think the WWE Universe thought too much of it," says Styles. "So they made it easy for expectations to be broken, like, 'Oh, wow, that was a lot better than I thought it was going to be.' It showed another side of Shane McMahon and what he could do and what he was capable of, and we were able to capitalize on everything we were able to do in there. For us, it was easy to go in and have the match of the night because we were first. And so now everybody has to keep up with us, and I was going to do my best to make sure that was difficult for everybody else. That's my job as a performer: to go in and steal the show. Despite the guidelines we had — you can't go here, you can't do that, we're using that move someplace else on the card — we went out there and tore it up without hurting anybody else's matches, and at the same time, we went out there trying to steal the show."

One of the reasons for Styles's success, he explains, is that he doesn't care about wins or losses, especially when it comes to a big event like *WrestleMania*. "You've already won, because you're at *WrestleMania*. That's the difference. At the end of the night, I don't want you to think about who won or lost, I want you to go, 'Holy cow, what an amazing match that was, I did not expect that.' I want to be the match that they want to see, and I want to pay them back by delivering the best match possible. So to me, the wins or the losses don't matter — it's about the wow factor.

"*WrestleMania* is so much bigger than I ever imagined before I joined WWE. When you're with a different company, you think that you're competing with them, and I know this from experience. You think we're getting closer, or momentum is heading our way, but then you look at the company from a worldwide perspective, and not just *WrestleMania*, but WWE is so much bigger than anyone can imagine.

There was a time when I was working with TNA, and they made all their money from another country, I think it may have been India. Now you think about how many countries WWE is in, and it's just ridiculous. So it's much bigger than I ever could've imagined, on every level. Nothing even comes close to WWE, and you may not even know this until you come here and you see it for yourself. You realize how much you're recognized now being in WWE as opposed to being that TNA guy or even a guy from Japan. When I used to come home through immigration, people would ask what were you doing overseas, and I'd say I was a wrestler, and they'd always say, 'Oh, like WWE?' And I'd be like, 'Yeah, like WWE.' Everything is referenced to WWE.

"And then you get to *WrestleMania*, and you're sitting in the back and you're seeing this crowd, this sea of people, literally, it's the most amazing thing I've ever seen. Unfortunately, when I step up on the stage and I make my entrance, they all fade away. It's like I don't see anybody. I have this tunnel vision and even when I'm looking at them, I don't see these people as much as I want to. Even when I slide in the ring and do my thing, I can't even see my own family because I'm trying to take in everybody at the same time. It's just amazing, the amount of people who are surrounding you and are interested in what you're doing, and so much so that you don't even hear them. At *WrestleMania 32* in Texas, I couldn't tell if anybody was enjoying me and Chris Jericho because all of the sound went straight up, it didn't surround us. That's how big that stadium was, I couldn't hear anything. In a stadium built for that many people, the acoustics of the building force the sound straight up, which is great for football because even with that many people cheering, the Dallas players can hear their quarterback calling the plays. But for professional wrestling, where we're trying to play off the fact that people are responding to what we're doing, it makes it tough. We would do a move, hear nothing, and be like, 'Well, that sucks.' I had to watch it back on video before I knew, okay, they did respond to this spot, I had no idea while it was happening live."

After Styles's victory over Shane McMahon, he moved on to a

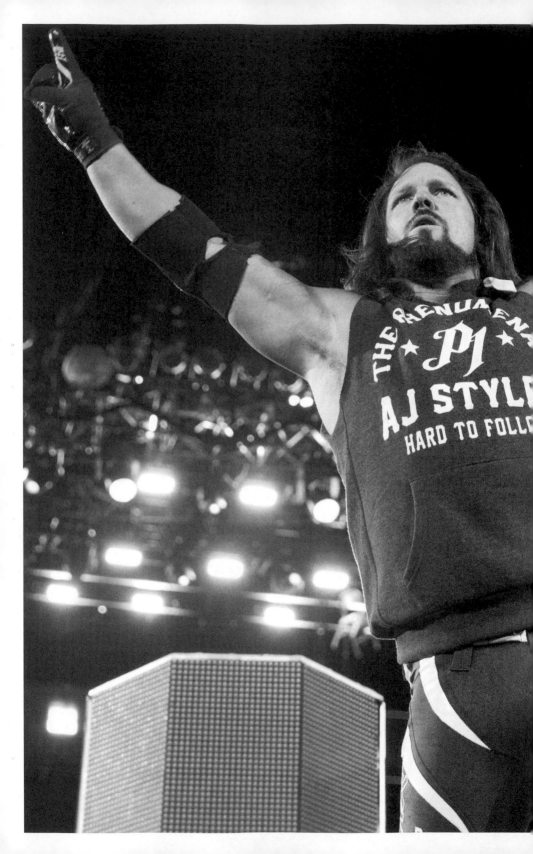

rivalry with Kevin Owens for the United States Championship, and the *SmackDown* star even appeared on the TLC *Raw* pay-per-view, subbing in for a sick Bray Wyatt to take on Finn Bálor in under a week's notice. "Things change, and you have to be prepared to change with them," says Styles. "We are professionals. This is what we do. There's not going to be any whining or complaining from me because you never know what will come from each and every opportunity. Creative thinks they know where they're going, maybe they have an idea, but things change so quickly and so often, you have to be prepared for everything. They give the WWE Universe what they want to see, and sometimes that means drastically changing where they're going in the storyline.

"I have to be ready to go where they want to take me, but there wasn't even a couple of days to figure out what to do. We texted, that's about it. As far as what we were going to do in the match, we didn't even talk about it until we got to the show, and I got to the show late because I was in South America. But you have two professionals in there who have been doing it for years, and we wanted to put on the best match we could, both for ourselves, for WWE, and for the WWE Universe. So it wasn't difficult to put together at all, it was easy and it was fun, and the crowd loved it. It was exactly what it needed to be."

And that adaptable mentality came in handy only a few weeks later, as again Creative pivoted directions, and on the November 7 episode of *SmackDown LIVE*, Styles defeated Jinder Mahal to capture the WWE Championship. This not only wiped out Mahal's dreams of main-eventing *WrestleMania 34* against John Cena, it also dramatically changed the main event of *Survivor Series*, where the champion versus champion main event now featured the never-before-seen dream match between Styles and "The Beast" Brock Lesnar — a match that saw suplexes, flying elbows, and the most devastating escape from the calf-crusher Styles has ever felt. And while the Phenomenal One lost via the F5, his fearlessness and ability to draw the best out of Brock shined the spotlight firmly on Styles, with Lesnar's advocate Paul Heyman cutting a promo backstage afterward, offering high praise for both the match and Styles himself. "If

you're not an AJ Styles fan, you shouldn't even be watching WWE," said Heyman. "He's everything that Shawn Michaels and Bret Hart and Ric Flair were to their generation, and he's updated it."

Post-Lesnar, Styles already has an opponent in mind for *WrestleMania 34*, but it will take some twists in the storyline to get there, including a win for his dream opponent at *Royal Rumble*. "If I had to book my story, I would be your WWE Champion going into *WrestleMania*, telling you that I want this match to happen on United States soil, not in Japan this time. My hometown, not his, and I want Shinsuke Nakamura," says Styles. "We had three or four days to build up Finn Bálor and AJ Styles, which is nothing in terms of building up a match — and the crowd went nuts for the match. So what would they do if we had me defend the title at *WrestleMania* against Shinsuke, and we had weeks, even months to build it. It would be incredible."

Almost as incredible as the fantasy match that Styles tried to put in place before *WrestleMania 33*. It's a match played out in video games and in the minds of the WWE Universe whenever they talk about dream matches, and according to Styles, he attempted to make the dream a reality in early 2017. "This all came about at last year's *Rumble*," explains Styles. "I brought up Shawn Michaels as my dream opponent. I asked, 'Has anybody talked to Shawn lately? Can we ask him? Worst he could say is no.' So the call was made, but he did say no.

"When I talked to Shawn about the match, he made a lot of good points. First of all, he had retired. That's a great thing, when a man keeps his word to stay retired, I appreciate that. Secondly, who would benefit if Shawn came back? If I beat him or he beats me, who would that benefit? Why not go out on top like Shawn Michaels did? He had one of the greatest matches of all time against Undertaker, and what a way to retire. That's the way you go out. I have nothing but respect for Shawn, and I appreciate him even talking to me to say no. The unfortunate thing is, I never got the opportunity to learn from Shawn Michaels. That's something I would've loved to have done."

CHAPTER 15
Imminent Deletion

DECEMBER 4, 2017: *MONDAY NIGHT RAW*

Matt Hardy is a master of reinvention. From The Hardy Boyz reign as tag team champions to the debut of Matt Hardy: Version 1, Hardy always seems to be one step ahead of the game. But in 2016, Hardy outdid even himself, bleaching part of his hair blond and introducing the wrestling world to the unpredictable and outlandish madman known as "Broken" Matt Hardy. The insane (and insanely captivating) storyline invited the audience inside the Hardy Compound. Complete with intoxicating piano playing, Matt's brother Jeff transforming into Brother Nero, a drone (Vanguard 1) that acts as the compound's head of security, Hardy's son playing the role of King Maxel alongside Hardy's wife (in both storyline and real life) Queen Rebecca, and Hardy's father-in-law taking on the role of loyal groundskeeper/henchman Senor Benjamin. Hardy created a universe on TNA television unlike anything ever seen. Specials like "Delete or Decay" and "Total Nonstop Deletion" became must-see TV, attracting millions of viewers online and igniting one of the most viral movements the sport has ever seen.

But when Matt and Jeff's TNA contract expired in 2017, The Hardy Boyz shocked the WWE Universe with their surprise return at *WrestleMania 33*. However, due to legal issues over who exactly owned the rights to the Broken Universe, the brothers were back to being the team from the Attitude Era, not the duo of Broken Brilliance fans had expected. "When my brother Jeff and I were at TNA, I started doing something that was very different. A character that is much larger than life, almost supernatural," explains Matt. "It is a throwback to the older days when wrestling had more character-driven personas. The Broken Matt Hardy character became so strong, that even my brother stopped being just Jeff Hardy, he became Brother Nero, Nero being his middle name. A new company bought the company we were working for, and they were going through a lot of changes, and they were downsizing, and we had been offered pretty good deals to stay, but there were other guys who were in the mix and we heard they were trying to undercut them in terms of money. We knew there was an opportunity to return home to WWE."

Matt and Jeff were contacted by Triple H, who eventually put them in touch with Vince McMahon and Head Producer/Ring Agent Michael Hayes, working out a deal for their return. But before *WrestleMania 33* arrived, the team decided to create a distraction so the WWE Universe couldn't predict the timetable of their return. "During that whole month of March, myself and my brother actually went to another promotion, Ring of Honor, and became their tag team champions, and we were involved in a really hot rivalry there with a tag team called The Young Bucks," says Matt. "We thought, and Triple H agreed with us, that wrestling in Ring of Honor would be a good way to create a diversion or create a smoke screen so people would be surprised when we showed up at *WrestleMania*. We told people that we were committed to Ring of Honor, and in all of our interviews, we were stringing people along that we were going to stay with Ring of Honor for a certain amount of time. The only thing that maybe gave it away to some of the diehard fans is that we dropped the titles in a Ladder Match the night before *WrestleMania*, in Lakeland, which was only about an hour away from where *WrestleMania 33* was being held in Orlando. We showed up that next day at *WrestleMania*, getting there the segment before our match started, and we snuck into the building and into Gorilla, wearing hoodies and everything so nobody would see us, and, literally, the first time being in front of the masses, that sea of humanity, was when we made our entrance to go out to the ring. The word is used a lot, but it was absolutely exhilarating. There was just such a tangible feel to the energy the crowd gave us. It's hard to describe it as anything else but intoxicating. It was the most amazing feeling and reaction I've ever had in my career. It was very, very special."

And while the WWE Universe saw the old-school Hardy Boyz run to ringside, they began Broken Universe chants like "Brother Nero" and "Delete! Delete! Delete!" "It made me proud because it shows that the fans who come to *WrestleMania* are some of the most diehard fans," says Matt. "It shows how society and our world has changed thanks to social media and various video platforms. Out stuff didn't become popular because of TNA, because in the grand scheme of things, it's such a small company, such a small, small platform. But after things like 'The Final Deletion' and 'Total Nonstop Deletion' went on YouTube and all of the different video platforms available, they got millions and millions of views. It became viral, and that's how it crossed over to all wrestling fans. When we came out in front of the WWE Universe at *WrestleMania 33*, you could see thousands of people doing the delete taunt, you could hear people chanting, 'Brother Nero!' and I can't tell you how ecstatic I was because it was so flattering and it was so humbling, and it just made me proud that these fans were appreciating our hard work from other places."

Behind the scenes, Matt was still negotiating to retain the rights to the Broken Gimmick, but until the legal battle was over, he was unable to use those characters on WWE TV. "That year that we did it in TNA, my brother and I paid for so many of the shoots that happened on our property, and there were so many things that we created — it was our brainchild," says Matt. "Literally, they had one guy, Jeremy Borash, who would come out and say we need twenty minutes for the show, and then we'd determine whatever the content was going to be."

While the legal battle continued, Matt introduced a new version of the Broken character on *Raw*, Woken Matt Hardy, in a hilarious back and forth video with former WWE Champion Bray Wyatt, where Hardy proclaimed, "Due to my condition, I have laid dormant inside this vessel called Matthew Hardy, but now, thanks to the consumer of terrestrial entities [Wyatt], I have been Woken . . . Bray Wyatt, you have left me no choice. I sentence you to deletion!" The video ended with the two rivals trading laughs like only two lunatics can, capturing perfectly in under two minutes the *Raw* insanity and strange charm of Hardy's new universe.

"It eventually got to the point where the person who was trying to block us from taking the Broken Universe to WWE was fired from the company, and I spoke with the owner, Ed Nordholm, and we worked out all of the terms and it's all good," says Hardy, of the legal battle. "Ironically, it was right after we started doing Woken Matt Hardy in WWE that I got the rights to the Broken Universe, but now it's going to be very cool because I can continue to incorporate elements from the Broken Universe into the new Woken Universe in WWE. The thing that is amazing about Broken Matt Hardy or Woken Matt Hardy is that there is no barometer, there are no boundaries. We can go anywhere and get away with anything. It's just fun. At its core, sports-entertainment and wrestling is supposed to be fun, it's supposed to be an escape from reality, and nothing is more fun than Woken Matt Hardy.

"When you're with WWE, obviously, Vince is going to have the final say on everything. It's been great, because even when I spoke to him and explained the backstory of the Broken Matt Hardy character — what his motivations were, what made him what he is — Vince was very open to saying, 'Okay, well, let's work together on this thing.' Even when I speak on *Raw*, they'll give me a framework, then I'll add words or phrases that I want in there. Vince still has the final say, but I get a ton

of input, more than other people get. And I wholeheartedly believe we will start to see elements from the Broken Universe on *Raw*, and from what I understand, we're going to start heading down that path soon. I have my fingers crossed and hopefully everything works out because all of those characters — like Queen Rebecca playing the piano and King Maxwell and Senor Benjamin — should have all been monetized, but TNA didn't have the resources to capitalize on any of it. In WWE, we could just do vignettes and different shots from my home, and those characters can exist in the Hardy Compound, and there would be a ton of merchandising and toys you can sell. These are monetized characters with a loyal following, so I believe WWE is looking to take advantage of that and incorporate them into upcoming storylines."

Hardy also hopes to continue playing to fans on the internet. In TNA, he took hilarious shots at "Mr. Meekmahan" and "The man with three Hs," and these moments helped Hardy's videos go viral. "The most interesting thing I tried to do was play to the narrative of the internet, and I think that's why it became so popular," says Hardy. "Vince McMahon made sports-entertainment what it is today, and anyone who is involved in it has to appreciate that and owes him a debt for what he has accomplished, but the internet acts like he's a megalomaniac who gets talent from another territory and immediately tries to bury it. They think he's out of control, so I just played up that narrative. Same thing with Triple H. Triple H has been absolutely incredible to work with since I've come back. Getting our piano music with a little trance-vibe to it, he hooked that up. He's been absolutely phenomenal. But online, the narrative is how he brings talent in only to beat them and embarrass them and how he always needs to stay strong. So I just played off those narratives. That made it very easy, and it became a fun thing, especially for those diehard fans. It was cathartic, getting to share their jokes on television. At some point, I spoke to Hunter about it, and he giggled a little bit, so there are more things I have in mind along those lines that I want to bring out. I want to play off the narratives that the internet buys into or believes. To me, that is part of the charm of the Broken/Woken Universe."

And with the Woken Universe debut, Hardy hopes to add longevity to his already multiple-decade career. "One of my successes in the business and having longevity is being able to adapt and evolve and change," says Hardy. "Considering that I've been doing this for twenty-five years now, taking on a more character-driven persona is going to benefit me in the long run. People are looking for more entertaining qualities coming out of the character as opposed to me being pushed off a fourteen-foot ladder and going through four tables on the floor. So this character enables me to continue to do what I love doing. If I need to get in the ring and kick ass and have a killer match, I can still do it, but I can't bounce back as fast as I could ten or fifteen years ago. That's just the reality of aging. That's why I try to stay ahead of the curve, changing the way I work and changing my character. As opposed to being an athletic force, I'm now more of a personality-driven force."

A personality force who hopes to see his run against Wyatt last long after *WrestleMania 34*. With Brother Nero scheduled to return from injury around *WrestleMania*, Matt would love to see how the three characters will interact. "I'm not one hundred percent certain, but either I will face Bray Wyatt, or Bray Wyatt will be with me and will be Woken," explains Hardy. "When it's all said and done, and I don't know if it's going to happen before *WrestleMania* or after *WrestleMania*, but I'm going to bring Bray Wyatt into the light." Hardy then turned on the switch to his Woken voice. "We got to wake him up. Sister Abigail must be deleted."

CHAPTER 16
Rumble, Young Woman, Rumble

DECEMBER 18, 2017: *MONDAY NIGHT RAW*

It's Absolution facing off against Sasha Banks, Bayley, and Mickie James in the *Monday Night Raw* main event. The two teams brawl back and forth until Mandy Rose and Sonya Deville beat down Sasha Banks with a barrage of fists. The referee attempts to step in, but when he can't get the women to stop punching, he disqualifies Absolution and awards the match to Banks, Bayley, and James. But the action is just getting started as Rose and Deville hold Banks up with Paige ready to add to the mayhem, when Nia Jax storms to the ring with an Absolution ass-kicking on her mind. Jax then hoists both Rose and Deville on her back at the same time to deliver a thunderous double Samoan drop. Paige then attacks Jax from behind, chop-blocking her knee and signaling for the rest of Absolution to continue the triple team. The rest of *Raw*'s women had seen enough, however, as the locker room empties and a huge brawl erupts that includes everyone from Alexa Bliss to Asuka.

All action ceases a minute later, however, as Stephanie McMahon's music hits and the *Raw* Commissioner struts down to the ring. The

Raw women gather around as McMahon says she has an announcement to make. "Three years ago, a revolution was started in WWE, led by all of the women in this ring, all of the women on *SmackDown LIVE*, and every single woman to ever step foot inside the ring including the Fabulous Moolah and the great Mae Young. And all of you turned that revolution into an evolution. Because of you, the Diva's Division became the Women's Division. You became the Superstars and the headliners, main-eventing just like the guys on *Monday Night Raw, SmackDown LIVE, NXT*, pay-per-views and blowing the roof off this joint. Because of you, we had the first ever women's Hell in a Cell Match. Because of you we had the first ever women's Money in the Bank Ladder Match. And just two weeks ago, women competed inside the ring in the Middle East for the first time in WWE, for the Women's Championship. And what was the chant, Sasha, what was the chant? 'This is hope!' You saw tears in the eyes of little girls sitting ringside because you inspired those little girls. All of you have inspired people all over the world with your courage, with your passion, with your unbridled talent. But that's not enough. What do you say, ladies, you want to make history once again? Do you people want to see these women make history once again? Then on January twenty-eighth, the road to *WrestleMania* kicks off in Philadelphia, Pennsylvania, and we will have for the very first time an all-women's Royal Rumble Match!"

The crowd starts chanting, "Yes! Yes! Yes!" followed by "You deserve it!" Tears could be seen from the women in the ring, along with genuine smiles as they hugged in celebration. For months, rumors and whispers circulated that this could happen, but no talent was told of the announcement until McMahon entered the ring and grabbed the mic. The look of shock and happiness was pure as the Women's Division was told the groundbreaking news at the same time as the audience, leading to one of the most memorable moments of the year.

"I was standing there, waiting to hear, and when she announced it, I got emotional because this is something I always wanted to do, not just with the girls but with the guys too," says Nia Jax. "Since we never had one before, when she announced it, that was my real reaction, like, 'Holy crap! The first Women's Royal Rumble!"

Immediately, though, the moment also led to endless speculation about who would actually appear in the 30-women, over-the-top-rope Rumble. Would legends like Trish Stratus or Lita appear? Women from NXT? Women from the Mae Young Classic? Could Carmella win the Royal Rumble, lose at *WrestleMania*, then cash in her Money in the Bank contract for an immediate rematch? And what about Ronda Rousey? Ever since the staredown between the Four Horsewomen at the Mae Young Classic, the WWE Universe has been waiting on word of a Rousey signing. Would the Rumble finally be her time to debut?

"I'd love to have her," says Roman Reigns. "I think she's great. She has a big name; she has a sports, fighting background; and I think she would definitely pick this up very quickly just based on her physical background and her athletic nature. Right now, we're highlighting the women. They're no longer Divas. If I say Diva, one of them might slap me. So to me, it fits perfectly to add another strong woman to an already strong division. It makes so much sense, if she's into it. I don't sign people, but if I could be responsible for signing Ronda Rousey, I'll take it."

Braun Strowman offered a different take. "There's no arguing that she's one of the baddest females on the planet," he says. "But at the same time, the women that I work with are some really tough women. I see them day in and day out, and that's the difference a lot of people don't understand about WWE versus UFC. They fight once every six months. We fight four nights a week and travel all over the world. We do things like compete in *Monday Night Raw*, hop on a red-eye at 10:30 p.m., land at 9:35 a.m Wednesday morning in New Zealand, perform four hours later, sleep for a few hours, then jump on a flight from New Zealand to Australia and perform again. We do that four nights a week all over the world. If Ronda joins full-time, it will be interesting to see if she could hold it together to fight more than just once every six months."

Former Women's Champion Sasha Banks takes Strowman's statement a little further. "To me, if you want to be a part of this, you have

to earn it. If you want to join this crazy world of wrestling, go out and train, get a tryout, hope to get signed, and then try to make your way through NXT. There are millions of women who want this more and who want to come out and do the exact same thing, and we already have so many amazingly talented women down in NXT, so I'm not here for someone to just walk in and take a spot. You've got to earn your spot just like everybody else. That's what I have to say about it."

Banks, whose "Legit Boss" character has exploded on the pop-culture scene, sees the influence the women of WWE have, and a Royal Rumble win would solidify her spot not only for another shot at the Women's Championship but for what she hopes is a main-event spot at *WrestleMania*. "We're legit getting over, we're legit taking over, and we're having all of these history making moments. We're doing all of these first-time-ever matches and moments, and it's almost becoming the norm, where it's not like, 'Look, it's the first time a woman did this or that,' it's more like, 'Look at what the women are doing.' We're doing the exact same thing as the guys. We're having these main-event moments, we're having the same match stipulations as the guys, so any-thing is possible. There's this beautiful change happening in the world where the women are taking over and we're doing everything equal to the guys. Whether it's this year or next year or a few years from now, women main-eventing *WrestleMania* is definitely going to happen.

"All you have to do is look into the crowd to see the change that's happening. It's honestly the best feeling ever when you see little girls dressed as you. You're seeing it so much more. You used to see little boys do it before, but now you see these young females whose eyes light up — that's legit the best feeling in the world. Being a wrestling fan, you want to watch characters who are larger than life — you want to dress like them and be like them. So whenever I thought about being in WWE, I knew I had to establish a look, a statement where people recognize me right away, whether it's the colorful hair or the blinged-out jewelry or the flashy outfit. When I'm walking down the aisle, I can see things flashing, and I'm like, 'Oh, that's my ring they're wearing.'

It's awesome. I want to be a role model for these young women, to let them know that they can do anything, and anything is possible. When I got signed to NXT, I could only dream of where I am now.

"All of the women are so much bigger than they were just a few years ago. Just not being called Divas anymore, being called Superstars, and not having the Divas title but having the Women's Championship, it all means so much. Now we have multiple women's storylines and all of these first-ever type matches, it truly is amazing. But what's funny is, I wrote it all down in a notebook before I even started. I wrote down that I wanted to be the best in the world, and through hard work and perseverance and God blessing us, we're making it happen. We're hoping to inspire young women and hoping to make it easier for the next group of women who want to be in WWE. I've been in WWE for five years, been on the main roster for two and half years, and the journey here was long and hard, but we're still here and we're still trying to make things happen — we're still trying to break down doors. It's just a beautiful journey, and I'm enjoying the process. When young women look back at me, I hope they say, 'Wow, Sasha Banks made this happen, or Charlotte made this happen, or Bayley made this happen, and if they did it, then I can do it too.'"

If Banks doesn't win the Royal Rumble, she has another dream match in mind. "My dream match is main-eventing *WrestleMania* against Bayley. Whoever I'm in the storyline with, I just want to make it the best possible. It can honestly be anyone, because anytime I'm in the ring, I'm ready to steal the show."

It's a match Bayley would love to pursue as well, but her first choice is a showdown between the dueling Four Horsewomen factions. "Honestly, I have so many dream *WrestleMania* matches," she says. "One of them is to do another Fatal 4-Way between myself, Becky, Sasha, and Charlotte that we did in *NXT TakeOver*. Another one is a singles match with Sasha Banks. Leading up to *WrestleMania 34*, what I really want is the Four Horsewomen versus the Four Horsewomen. You saw the Four Horsewomen of UFC hanging around the *Mae Young*

Classic, so I just think it would be kind of cool to welcome them in for one night only and see how they handle business in *WrestleMania*."

These are just some of the ideas Bayley plans to pitch to Creative leading into the big show. "They love ideas," she explains. "It's always awesome to sit with Creative and talk about your ideas, their ideas, and then to be able to put stuff together so you can create this vision that you may have or they may have. They're really good at accepting your ideas, whether they end up going with it or not. Sometimes you have an idea of where you might be going, but it's usually day to day. It's so busy and there are so many people we work with, it's hard to keep track of everybody, but for *WrestleMania* you might not find out what you're doing until the day of."

And like Banks, Bayley is left in awe by the number of girls in the crowd who are starting to mimic their every move, right down to the ponytail. "It's really crazy, and it's something I don't know if I'll ever get used to, in a good way, because that used to be me when I was a kid," says Bayley. "I used to dress like Lita, and I'd wear the baggy pants and the choker necklaces and I'd cut my T-shirts to look cool, just because I wanted to look like her. Now I see girls, and even if they have only a side ponytail and a headband, I know they're representing me, and that's what I've always wanted. I want to have kids experience what I experienced when I went to these shows; I want kids to feel the same way I felt. And now we see girls dressed as all of the women, from Carmella to Sasha Banks to Alexa Bliss, and it's cool to see the influence the women Superstars have over these girls now. That's the type of influence that women like Lita had on us years ago."

And with the Women's Royal Rumble only a month away, there's a chance Bayley will be able to repay Lita's influence with a hug inside the ring, or maybe even toss her idol over the top rope. Anything to get back to *WrestleMania*, a stage Bayley debuted on at *WrestleMania 33*. "I was weirdly calm going into it, and I think it's because I had Sasha and Charlotte, who I had grown up with a lot the last two years and in NXT, along with me," she says. "I felt very comfortable knowing that they were going to be there. But at the same time, it was my first *WrestleMania*, and I had all of my family and friends there, and I was the champion going in, so I almost felt like it was all too good to be true. It was my first year in WWE, so I really didn't expect to be in my first *WrestleMania*, and I really didn't think I'd be walking in as champion, so I just kept thinking something bad was going to happen since everything had been so good building to that moment. Luckily nothing happened. The worst thing was I slipped on my entrance. I slipped on one of the inflatables, and I thought everything was going downhill, but luckily everything worked out fine and I ended up coming out victorious in the match. It was a lot of hard work going into the event. I've never worked out that hard or dieted that hard going into any match, so that was a little stressful, but once I got behind the curtain, I was ready.

"The railway was so long in Orlando that I had time to soak it all in. It was so hard to actually hear people because it was so big, it was outdoors. I was on cloud nine — I couldn't believe it was actually happening — so I think I canceled out some of the noise, but when I got to the ring, that's when it hit me. That's when I could hear people. Because you're right there with the people in the front row. When I started to watch the other girls do their entrances, that's when I started getting emotional. My family was in the front row, so I knew I couldn't look at them. I was trying to look around and look at other people so I could dry my tears before the match started."

PART TWO
Intermission

WrestleMania Moments

Your favorite Superstars' all-time favorite *Mania* matches and moments.

CHARLOTTE FLAIR, *WrestleMania XXIV*

"It was the last time my family was all together to see my dad. You kind of felt that, as a whole, that was my dad's weekend. You saw all of the 'Thank You, Ric' shirts in the crowd and the WWE Universe was so emotionally invested in that match. It was unbelievable. It was also the first time I really realized what my dad meant to the industry. I was blown away. From his retirement to the moments right after he wrestled Shawn Michaels, everybody was on their feet crying. Grown men were crying in the stadium because he retired. It was unbelievable. I don't think I've ever had a moment like that or have seen someone earn that much respect from the audience before."

AJ STYLES, *WrestleMania XII*

"When Shawn Michaels did that crazy entrance, coming down on a cable. That was the coolest entrance I've seen, so I'd want to do something crazy like that. I'd love to try it at a *WrestleMania* coming up."

BRAUN STROWMAN, *WrestleMania III*

"When Hogan body slammed Andre the Giant. There isn't a more iconic moment out there in our sport."

ROMAN REIGNS, *WrestleMania IX*

"For me, it was bittersweet. It was actually the Ceasars Palace *WrestleMania* where Yokozuna won the title, but then Hogan ran down and won it from him. I've always been a fan of Hogan, my family has always been really close to Hogan, my father and uncle rode with him and everything, but we were so happy for Yokozuna. And then here comes Hogan to take the title off of him. As a child, I was just infuriated, but it took my dad and uncle to explain that it was just a business, and it was actually a great honor for Yokozuna to not only beat Bret Hart but to be able to put the championship on Hogan, the greatest of all time. It's funny because I didn't understand it back then. I didn't understand why my dad was gone. I don't understand why he couldn't just come home for a month. There were a lot of things you didn't understand as a child, but for me now, walking in their footsteps and being in their shoes, I have such a greater respect for what they went through, what's really going on, and what we're doing out here in the ring, trying to achieve these goals we all have for our families. I'm glad now to have that hindsight. Things are a lot clearer now."

KEVIN OWENS, *WrestleMania 25*

"To this day, I think the best *WrestleMania* match of all time — and I don't know how anyone can say that this isn't the best *WrestleMania* match of all time — Undertaker versus Shawn Michaels. It's just a masterpiece. I wasn't there live, but I watched it from home and it was so incredibly well done, and everything was just so perfect. It was two legends putting on an incredible match. That's the top of the list, and I don't know if it will ever be topped. There are so many *WrestleMania* moments that stick with you through the years. I saw Kurt Angle and Shawn Michaels live at *WrestleMania 21*, and that was an absolutely unbelievable match as well. I was at *WrestleMania X8* for Rock and Hogan, and the crowd for that match was just so loud. Watching Steve Austin win the title at *WrestleMania XIV*, Shawn winning the title at *WrestleMania XII*, those are just a few of the moments that stick with me."

MATT HARDY, *WrestleMania IV, WrestleMania X*
"Growing up, two things really stood out: one is when "Macho Man" Randy Savage won the WWE Championship. He was always my guy, so I was so excited to see him succeed and win. The other was the Shawn Michaels versus Razor Ramon Ladder Match. Obviously, that was very influential in my career, and it was instrumental in motivating us to start doing Ladder Matches, which led to the whole TLC craze. It's incredibly humbling when some of the younger Superstars come up to me and say, 'Oh, man, I loved you and your brother,' and they talk about how influential our TLC Matches were. These guys were just fans back then, and now I work with them. It's funny because it reminds me of how I got to work with Undertaker and Shawn Michaels. Obviously, before I was in the business, I was a fan of their work and what they did, so later getting the chance to work with them was hugely inspirational and such a cool thing. It's weird. It's like a role reversal, because now I'm that guy that the younger guys want to work with. It's very cool."

JASON JORDAN, *WrestleMania X*
"As the youngest of four boys, and being part of a brotherhood, the most influential *WrestleMania* match of all time was when Bret Hart faced his brother Owen. That match stood out to me as a moment where I definitely wanted to be a part of WWE and become a wrestler at some point. The bond that they showed as brothers that night really stood out strong. To top it off, Owen won! Score one for the younger brother."

JIMMY USO, *WrestleMania IX, WrestleMania 23*
"I really enjoyed when Yoko beat Bret for the title, but then Hogan

came out and beat him for the title. I also loved when my uncle Umaga had the hair versus hair match against Bobby Lashley. You go back and watch that one, it was a hell of a match."

JEY USO, *WrestleMania IX*
"My dad was on the card against the Steiner Brothers, and I remember him saying that his feet were burnt because the mat was so hot from the sun. That's a cool little fact right there."

DANIEL BRYAN, *WrestleMania XII*
"Whenever people think of their favorite matches, it's also tied into your emotions at the time you're watching the match or anything significant happening in your life around that time. Growing up, I was a huge wrestling fan, but I couldn't afford the pay-per-views until *WrestleMania XII*. I was working at McDonald's making $4.45 an hour, so I saved up money because I was so excited to see the Shawn Michaels versus Bret Hart Iron Man Match. To this day, if you watch it, it has that nostalgia of childhood, but they're also these two awesome performers. And I love long matches, so the fact it went over sixty minutes, it still makes me all kinds of happy and is my personal favorite *WrestleMania* match."

ELIAS, *WrestleMania 25*
"I got to see Shawn Michaels take on Undertaker live, in probably the greatest match of all time. I was there to feel those emotions from the crowd and to see that story play out. It was amazing."

RICOCHET, *WrestleMania XV*
"The Rock versus Steve Austin was my favorite match, even if I feel like Rock/Austin from *WrestleMania X-7* was their best match. Their match from *XV* was the match that made me want to be a wrestler. The match was so amazing, it inspired me to be where I'm at today."

Grown men were crying in the stadium because he retired. It was unbelievable. **CHARLOTTE FLAIR**

That was the coolest entrance I've seen . . . I'd love to try it at a WrestleMania. **AJ STYLES**

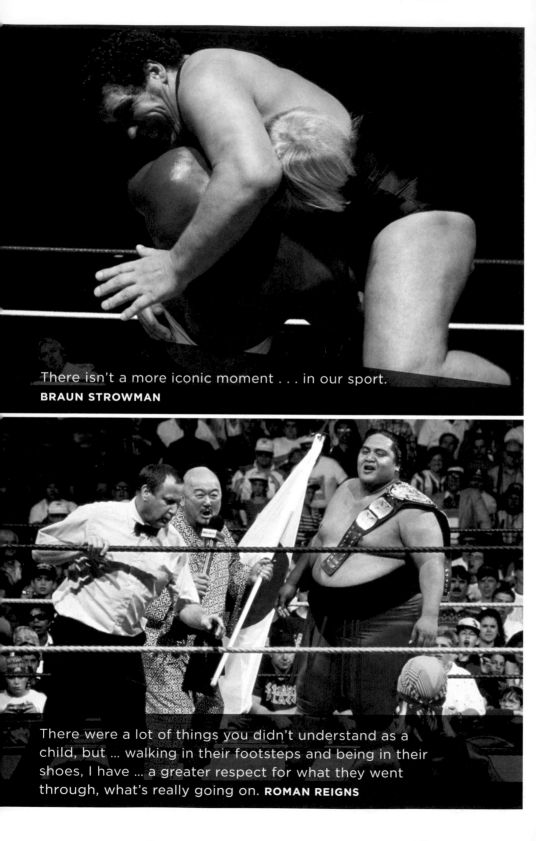

There isn't a more iconic moment . . . in our sport.
BRAUN STROWMAN

There were a lot of things you didn't understand as a child, but ... walking in their footsteps and being in their shoes, I have ... a greater respect for what they went through, what's really going on. **ROMAN REIGNS**

I think the best *WrestleMania* match of all time — and I don't know how anyone can say that this isn't the best *WrestleMania* match of all time — Undertaker versus Shawn Michaels. It's just a masterpiece. **KEVIN OWENS**

Obviously, before I was in the business, I was a fan
of their work and what they did, so later, getting the
chance to work with them was hugely inspirational.
MATT HARDY

That match stood out to me . . . I definitely wanted to be a part of WWE and become a wrestler. **JASON JORDAN**

You go back and watch . . . it was a hell of a match. **JIMMY USO**

I remember him saying that his feet were burnt because the mat was so hot from the sun. **JEY USO**

I was there to feel those emotions from the crowd and to see that story play out. It was amazing. **ELIAS**

To this day, if you watch it, it has that nostalgia of childhood, but they're also these two awesome performers. **DANIEL BRYAN**

The match was so amazing, it inspired me to be where I'm at today. **RICOCHET**

As a wrestling nerd, I appreciated the technical aspects of the match and the great storytelling that went along with it. Such a phenomenal match. **CESARO**

Bret Hart versus Steve Austin. . . That match is an absolute masterpiece. **SAMI ZAYN**

It was chaotic: Jimmy Hart got dragged into the ring, Brutus Beefcake came down and clipped Adonis's hair. It was . . . such a fun match to watch. **SHEAMUS**

The way the match played out and the atmosphere inside the stadium made it a lot of fun. **RANDY ORTON**

I thought it was done perfectly, and they both delivered, especially Hogan. **KURT ANGLE**

There are a lot of great matches that you watch in the moment, but that's the match you can watch ten, fifteen, a hundred times. **FINN BALOR**

You can see the tears in Ric's eyes, and I started tearing up, too. **NIA JAX**

CESARO, *WrestleMania X*

"Bret Hart versus Owen Hart. As a kid, I was a big Owen Hart fan, and I was on Owen's side leading up to the match. As a wrestling nerd, I appreciated the technical aspects of the match and the great storytelling that went along with it. Such a phenomenal match."

SHEAMUS, *WrestleMania III*

"The most entertaining match I've ever seen was Roddy Piper versus 'Adorable' Adrian Adonis. The match lasted only about five minutes, but the crowd was so into it. It was chaotic: Jimmy Hart got dragged into the ring, Brutus Beefcake came down and clipped Adonis's hair. It was just such a fun match to watch."

CEDRIC ALEXANDER, *WrestleMania X-7*

"The one moment that stands out is when Edge speared Jeff Hardy while he was hanging from the belt. That is a moment I'll never, ever forget. It was insane."

SAMI ZAYN, *WrestleMania 13*

"Bret Hart versus Steve Austin. That match is an absolute masterpiece. It made Steve Austin not only a star, but a star who went on to become a generation-defining star. The match is a true testament to Bret Hart and his ability."

RANDY ORTON, *WrestleMania X8*

"The Rock versus Hulk Hogan. I was there for that one and the crowd was so amazing. The way the match played out and the atmosphere inside the stadium made it a lot of fun."

KURT ANGLE, *WrestleMania X8*

"I loved the buildup and the match between The Rock and Hulk Hogan. I thought it was done perfectly, and they both delivered, especially Hogan. As limited as he was, it was a fun match to watch."

FINN BÁLOR, *WrestleMania XII*

"Shawn Michaels versus Bret Hart in the Iron Man Match. There are a lot of great matches that you watch in the moment, but that's the match you can watch ten, fifteen, a hundred times, and it still stands the test of time. It's by far my favorite *WrestleMania* match."

NIA JAX, *WrestleMania XXIV*

"One of my favorites is Shawn Michaels versus Ric Flair. When Shawn was like, 'I'm sorry, I love you,' how could you not feel the emotion of that moment? You can see the tears in Ric's eyes, and I started tearing up too."

PART TWO

2018

CHAPTER 17
Gold-Blooded

The *Monday Night Raw* 25th anniversary show started out with a stunner . . . make that three, as "Stone Cold" Steve Austin kicked it off by hitting a flurry of finishers on Shane and Vince McMahon, just for old time's sake, cracking open beer after beer, and dousing WWE ownership to the roar of the crowd. And the three-hour show was packed with nostalgia, from D-Generation X reuniting to pass the torch to the Bálor Club, complete with Too Sweet's all-around, to the return of Undertaker, giving hope to the WWE Universe that the Dead Man's career might not be so dead after all.

One of the most fun segments of the event was WWE legend Christian bringing back his Peep Show interview segment, with special guests Jason Jordan and Seth Rollins. It was just the latest spotlight for former amateur wrestling stud Jordan, whose whirlwind year had seen him elevated from American Alpha member, to Kurt Angle's son, to tag team champion alongside Seth Rollins (after a Dean Ambrose injury sidelined The Shield star). Jordan smirked as he soaked in the fans' scorn on *Raw 25*, making the Peep Show segment all his own thanks to his entitled and goofy persona playing into the crowd's chorus of boos, with statements like "My dad doesn't suck" and "Stand up and give my dad a big round of applause." Jordan stood up to lead the applause, and the crowd hated his every clap, just as he intended. The 29-year-old had them right where he wanted, and as his character continued to evolve throughout the year, it was very reminiscent of his on-screen father's personality throughout the Attitude Era.

To Jordan, the comparisons are beyond flattering, as he lists Angle as one of his favorite all-time talents. "I had different phases of who were my favorites," says Jordan. "Originally, I was an Ultimate Warrior fan, then I was a huge Curt Hennig ['Mr. Perfect'] fan. Kurt was another one of my all-time favorites, especially during the Attitude Era. Being an amateur wrestler, that resonated with me. But his personality and charisma and how incredible it was to see him go from this goofy, entertaining character to a badass killer was definitely something that resonated with me. I think there's going to be some similarities in how I'm portrayed. You might see me show my goofy side, but to keep growing, I have to show that killer that's in me. That has to come out in order to balance my character.

"I feel like when we get into this business, a lot of us are just looking for an opportunity. I've been given an opportunity, and I'm running with it as far as I can. Sink or swim, and I think I'm swimming pretty well right now. It feels great. This is pretty much what everybody asks for."

And according to everyone from Superstars like Roman Reigns to members of the creative team, Jordan is shaping up to become WWE's next big thing. The first step was separating him from American Alpha, in order to give him the spotlight on *Raw* in the Kurt Angle storyline. "Vince called me into the office one day and gave me the rundown of what we were going to do," says Jordan. "We were going to announce the following week on *Raw* that I was Kurt's son, and that was it. The rest is history." Jordan was told to keep the storyline secret, but he filled in Chad Gable so his American Alpha partner wasn't completely out of the loop. "We had to keep it a secret amongst ourselves," laughs Jordan.

One week later, Jordan was on TV next to one of his wrestling idols, introduced as Angle's son as Jordan's real family watched from home. "My parents are an incredible support system. They've been supportive of everything throughout my entire life, and now in sports-entertainment," says Jordan. "They've been incredible, and they definitely get it and help make it fun."

Jordan started amateur wrestling at age seven; he thought he was entering into some sort of kid's version of WWE but quickly found out he wouldn't be DDTing any opponents. "I started amateur wrestling thinking it was going to be like WWE," says Jordan. "I was the youngest of four boys, and they all watched wrestling, so it was grandfathered into the youngest — wrestling was just one of the things that we did. Obviously, amateur wrestling is slightly different than WWE, so when I showed up, I realized I couldn't just clothesline someone. But I loved amateur wrestling."

Amateur wrestling helped open the doors not only to Indiana University, where Jordan competed and was at one time ranked as the number two heavyweight in the nation, but to WWE as well. WWE scout Jerry Brisco spotted the young athlete and offered him a tryout. "A lot of guys who wrestled in college around that same time went the path of MMA, which was a thought in my mind at one point, but, honestly, WWE is what I wanted to do from the get-go," says Jordan. "I wasn't really aware of how possible it actually was, but I have a buddy who I wrestled with in college, and we'd joke about it, saying how awesome it would be if someone from WWE would see us amateur wrestling and sign us. Funny thing is, it actually worked out for me. That's basically where it all started."

Jordan's FCW tryout consisted of a week of training, learning the basics and what the Superstar describes as "the beginning stages and fundamentals in the ring." He was able to stretch his athletic

ability from there once he was officially signed. In FCW and then NXT, Jordan established himself as a tag team specialist, first teaming with CJ Parker to win the FCW Tag Team Championship, then teaming with Chad Gable and taking on the name American Alpha before defeating The Revival for the NXT Tag Team Championship. "When I first got into FCW, I thought singles was where it was at," says Jordan. "But after teaming with Chad Gable, I had such an amazing time being part of American Alpha that I definitely preferred tag team wrestling. It changed my mind. Being in the position that we were in with American Alpha and being in the title hunt a lot, it definitely put me in big-match situations that has helped out in my singles run right now. On top of that, Chad Gable is an incredible partner, one of the best you can ever ask for, and he always pushed me, he pushed himself, and we were competitors who always tried to make each other better. Now I'm enjoying my singles run as well, especially as my character development continues, but to be honest, I have a soft spot for tag team wrestling. It's always going to be something that stands out for me. There's a built-in story to tag team wrestling, and when you have two teams that gel well, it's an incredible story to tell and can make for some amazing matches."

Jordan, who is the first competitor to win the NXT, *Raw*, and *SmackDown* Tag Team Championships, stepped in for the injured Dean Ambrose on *Raw*'s Christmas episode to team with Seth Rollins, and the new team defeated The Bar to win the *Raw* tag team titles. "Look, nobody is going to be able to replace Dean Ambrose," says Jordan. "You can't just throw somebody into the mix and think that they are going to take his spot . . . it's just not going to happen. So I think you have to make the dynamic a little bit different, and the writing team has done a great job of that, and then when we put our own little flavor on the scenarios we're given, that's what we bring to the table when we're out there.

"Week by week, I'm taking what's given to me and I'm trying to put my own feel on it. I've gotten really involved with my character, and it has been a lot of fun, really getting invested. I think there are so many things that I've had to pull the reins back on and slowly assess where we were going with things, but it has been a lot of fun, just taking it week by week while putting my own little flavor on what I can. Hopefully there's more to come and it just continues to get better.

"I don't know if they'll fully allow me to put the tactical vest on yet. I guess that's one of the things you have to be gifted into. It wouldn't be as cool if I just did it myself. But I definitely feel like the guys see something in me that they can work with, and that's what we need in the long term, Superstars who we can all work with for years to come. It definitely helps that they've seen something in me, and I just need to continue to execute and learn everything I can from them. That's how we all get better. That's how we can live up to our potential. We need to get there together, and hopefully this ride will continue. As long as guys continue to see something in me, it's only going to help me. Seth has been in an incredible position for quite a long time now, being in the main-event picture, so he definitely offers an area of expertise about the business that will help move me to the next level. I know he's definitely trying to humble me and tell me that I still have a lot to learn, and he's right, I still do have a lot to learn. Hopefully he continues to help me grow not only as a singles competitor but as a competitor period."

Another Superstar who has been feeding Jordan advice is Kurt Angle. "Isn't that what a dad's supposed to do?" laughs Jordan. "Seriously, though, Kurt Angle is a great person to learn from, and one thing he told me is to take care of myself and take care of my body. We only have one body and — he would be a great example of this — when your body starts failing you, you can't do what we do week in and week out. I need to make sure I take care of myself, take care of my body, and that includes mental health as well. That's a big key to longevity — it's all about taking care of ourselves."

And while most of the WWE Universe assumes the Rollins/Jordan partnership will lead to a breakup worthy of a *WrestleMania* match, the creative team actually has something bigger in mind for the young

Superstar. "The original plan was actually going to be Rollins versus Ambrose," explains *Raw* writer Ed Koskey, "and when Ambrose was injured, at first we were thinking about doing Rollins versus Jordan, but then plans changed to Jordan versus Angle." That's right, an on-screen family rivalry between Jordan and his idol.

"Anything is possible," says Jordan when asked about the prospect of a match against Angle. "That's the great thing about going week to week: you never know what's going to happen. It would definitely be a shocker or a surprise if I did turn on him, but we will just have to wait and see. I think it would definitely make for an intriguing storyline. It could come from all sorts of directions, and I think it would add a nice little twist. It's definitely something I'd like to see happen eventually. My dream match would be for me to be teamed with Kurt at *WrestleMania* in some way, shape, or form. Whoever the opponent is, just being out there with Kurt would be a dream match onto itself. If either of those two things happen, I'd be happy."

CHAPTER 18
Yes! Yes! Yes! No!
No! No! Maybe?

JANUARY 28, 2018: *ROYAL RUMBLE*

The creative team had been scrambling behind the scenes for months writing and rewriting plans for *WrestleMania*, but to the WWE Universe, the on-screen road to *WrestleMania* truly begins at *Royal Rumble*. But what actually goes into planning the event? This year, producers had to plan out both the men's and women's Royal Rumbles, but according to *SmackDown* Vice President of Creative Brian James, aka the Road Dogg, it's actually one of the most fun matches to plan. James explains the match is not planned by the creative writing team but by producers such as Michael Hayes, who will work with Vince, and even a producer from NXT, in order to give the match fresh eyes. "You spend several days in a hotel conference room with a white board, thinking every scenario over," says James. "You pick out the thirty people, you pick out the order, and you come up with some interesting spots. I was there when we came up with Socko versus The Cobra with Mick Foley and Santino back in the day. It's nothing at all when you compare it to the big eliminations, but it's the little beats in there, several of those little beats that make the match memorable and provide that water-cooler talk.

"Writing that *Royal Rumble* and trying to continue that excitement for sixty minutes is a cool thing to do, especially when it works. And this year, we have two Rumbles. Producers are going back and forth, trying not to repeat spots, so we actually have a continuity guy assigned who knows what is going into all of the matches on the card, so he can say, 'You can't do that here, it's already being done in the other Rumble.' Sometimes, we need to decide which one is going to get to do it."

And while the epic wins for Shinsuke Nakamura and Asuka helped set up huge matches for *Mania*, one of the most shocking moments of the night was the debut of Ronda Rousey. Her signing has been whispered about for months, but both James and *Raw* Creative VP Ed Koskey said nobody on the creative team was told she was going to appear at the Rumble. "None of us from the creative team knew it was happening until we saw her walk out there," says Koskey. "Paul and Vince wanted to keep it super, super close to the vest, so we didn't know until we heard her music and saw her out there, pointing at the *WrestleMania* sign."

One surprise appearance that did not happen, however, was Daniel Bryan's rumored return to the ring. Before *Royal Rumble*, overseas betting sites saw Bryan's odds of winning the Rumble skyrocket, leading many to speculate that Bryan, who has been sidelined for over two years due to concussion issues, might have finally been cleared by WWE doctors to return. Bryan said he saw the rumors on Twitter and was completely baffled by how it started. "It was very, very strange because nothing had changed with my situation," says Bryan. "I'm still, to this day, not cleared to wrestle, so it was more perplexing, like, who are these people that are betting? The only thing I could think of is it was storyline driven, based on the idea of what we were doing with Shane and I, and us having some disturbances. Then I was also involved in the storyline with AJ, who is the champion, so in terms of plausibility, with the Royal Rumble winner getting a shot at the champion, and with the Royal Rumble Match always featuring surprises and secrets

and that sort of thing, someone must have thought it was in the realm of plausibility, and people took hold of it and started betting. I honestly have no idea how it got started or why it got started."

Bryan's status for the *Rumble* was never in play, but behind the scenes the performer has been working hard trying to get cleared in time for *WrestleMania*. "I've been pitching stories for stuff with Shane and me, and Sami Zayn and Kevin Owens. I tell them here's something we can do if I do get cleared, and I'm trying to get cleared, and then here are other things we can do if I don't get cleared." Bryan even worked out a storyline that he hopes to see play out after the *Rumble*, which would lead to his return match against longtime nemesis The Miz at *WrestleMania 34*. "I actually pitched an idea that would see Miz come back to *SmackDown* after the *Royal Rumble*," he explains. "Since I was doing things with Kevin Owens and Sami Zayn that was irritating Shane, I had pitched that Shane would bring Miz back to irritate me. That would lead to more Shane stuff with the three of us and then also give AJ a new challenger for the title. If I were to come back, a match with Miz would be hot."

"It's frustrating from a creative standpoint because it's in the medical field's hands," says James, when talking about possible matches for Bryan at *Mania*. "I would love to have him, from a creative standpoint, but as far as I know, as a dumb old wrestler and now a writer, I don't want to see him get injured further. But if he's good to go, I'd love to have him. Again, we're closing in on *Mania*, and I don't know if he's going to be cleared to work or not. I know they're trying to see what they can do, but until the doctors clear him, it would be a waste of time to put a bunch of creative energy in coming up with a bunch of storylines when you don't know the outcome. You might get there and then it doesn't happen, and then what? There have been so many times in the past where we got snakebit because they tell us someone is going to be cleared by a certain date, and then they're not, so we spent all this time writing a storyline, then the date gets pushed back and we're like, 'Crap!' That's when you switch courses mid-stream as far as storylines go. We try, from a creative standpoint, to let real-life situations like medical injuries or legal issues clear before we dive in and try to come up with a storyline. It's difficult, and it's extra difficult around *WrestleMania* season because everyone wants to be on the card and you want all your big stars to be on the grandest stage of them all."

But that hasn't stopped Bryan from continuing to pitch new storylines as he continues to see a slew of doctors in hopes of getting cleared. "Dr. Joseph Maroon is the head of medical with WWE, and you have to understand that concussions are not an objective issue. Right now, we can do very macroscopic studies of the brain, which means large-picture studies of how the brain is functioning. We cannot do microscopic functions of the brain. There is not a test that can determine whether someone has a tau protein in their brain. The tau protein in the brain is something that is associated with CTE [chronic traumatic encephalopathy]. Right now, we can only find that in people after they have passed away. Even though all of my brain scans, all of my MRIs, all of my EEGs, all of my neuropsychological testing has come back not only good but better than your average person, that doesn't mean that

I'm cleared. You have to think of this in terms of the neurologists who are seeing you. Just because these things come back clean doesn't mean that there's nothing, but that doesn't mean that there's something. And so, when you put it in that perspective, you can understand why someone like Dr. Maroon would say, 'In my judgment, in my estimation, I do not feel comfortable clearing you at this point.' But he also said, 'Listen, I'm not the sole authority on this.' There are a lot of people in the neurology field, and he gave me the names of the three neurologists who he most trusts in the United States, and I've seen all three of them and I've gotten cleared by all three of them. Does that change my situation? I don't know. This is a very fluid process. I've been cleared by all three neurologists, and then I've been sent to another few doctors, so I think in the next couple of weeks I will hear yay or nay whether or not they will clear me. That is the process I'm going through right now. In my buildup to *WrestleMania*, there is a lot of uncertainty, and my tie-in to *WrestleMania* is also my tie-in to coming back to WWE.

"In the meantime, I've still been in the storyline with Shane. But as far as I know, they don't know where this is all leading because a lot of it depends on the hope that I do get cleared, and if I do get cleared, what does it all mean? Does that mean me versus Shane? Does that mean Shane and I versus Sami and Kevin? Does it mean none of those things and something else entirely? I think from a talent perspective, unless you are cleared and a top guy, you know very little about where the storyline is going. I'm kind of a top guy, but I'm not cleared, so they're not counting on me being cleared in their buildup toward *WrestleMania*. I think one of the things that has frustrated people is whether or not we're building this dissension to lead to something. Are we doing it because there is this lull before the *Royal Rumble* and we needed captivating television? Here's an interesting, captivating thing that we may pay off or we may not pay off. We had some extremely captivating things between Miz and I that we never paid off. Because of what happened on *Talking Smack* between Miz and I last year, people expected that I was definitely coming back to do a *WrestleMania* match. But that didn't happen, nor was it ever close to happening. This year, we're closer. I've been pushing to make this happen and pushing the idea of getting cleared. If they're not going to clear me, then I need to start making plans for when my contract is up in September. Last year, I wanted to be cleared, but it didn't matter because I couldn't really do anything; I was under contract. This year, it's a little bit different because my contract is up, and if they're not going to clear me, I need to make other plans."

As he waits to learn his own *WrestleMania* fate, Bryan is super excited to see what Nakamura and Styles could do on the biggest show of the year. "There had been a brief altercation between Shinsuke and AJ at *Money in the Bank*, and the WWE Universe went crazy for it. It's something that especially our hardcore fanbase would like to see," says Bryan. "If you're familiar with wrestling outside of the United States, outside of WWE, AJ and Nakamura had an incredible match at New Japan, and I think the WWE Universe has realized how talented both of our Superstars are and would love to see that match. If you look at the *WrestleMania* card, there is always that one great work-rate match. I used to call it the Shawn Michaels match. It's the match where Shawn Michaels goes out and steals the show. It's weird that it's so late in the year and we have no idea what the card is, but it looks to me like AJ and Nakamura, when all is said and done, this is the match that people are going to look at and say, this is the great match.

"When Shinsuke first came to NXT, he wrestled Sami Zayn, and you saw this great blow-away match between Sami and Nakamura, and I think we're still waiting for that one blow-away match on the main roster because everyone knows it's there. Even some of the WWE Universe who aren't as hardcore and don't follow Japanese wrestling know it's there, and a match with AJ is something that can explode, especially with how great AJ has been. When you're looking at philosophies of wrestling, so many people have different opinions on what makes a great wrestling match, and it's subjective, but AJ checks off all of the boxes, especially in modern wrestling. He not only tells the old-school stories that you're used to — like a Ric Flair style of wrestling where the match is back and forth and the story is about heart and determination and all of that kind of stuff — his match against Brock is the perfect example of that — but he also incorporates modern moves that are not only exciting, they are very difficult to perform. The degree of difficulty of some of the moves he executes is off the charts and he makes it look like these moves could happen in a real fight. He does things that you normally only see from the cruiserweights. He's out there doing an inverted 450 splash, and from a technical standpoint, that's more difficult than a springboard 450 splash, but the average person might not realize that because it's so esthetically pleasing and so exciting."

The other match Bryan thinks has a chance to shine is Asuka versus Charlotte, but the match's greatness could be dependent on card placement and time allotted. "The thing you have to think of with every *WrestleMania* is how much time they get, how much focus they get on television, and their placement on the card," he explains. "The difference between a match being considered great and being considered okay has a lot to do with its placement on the card. If Charlotte versus Asuka is the second match and they're given fifteen minutes of ring time, I have no doubt that it will be awesome. If they are placed after Nakamura versus AJ Styles and it's after Ronda Rousey doing whatever she's doing and it's after they've seen ten million moves and the show is already six hours long and they go out there and do a fifteen-minute match, it might be very difficult for them to get the crowd. A lot of that is perception and placement and time. Likewise, if you go out there and you're originally allotted fifteen minutes of ring time, which at *WrestleMania* is about twenty minutes of total time when you add in entrances, but then you go to Gorilla and you're told that because everything is going long, you've been cut to twelve minutes total, then all of a sudden, you're not going to be as great as you thought because now you're talking about an eight-minute match. Then you're rushing through stuff and trying to do your best. I think AJ and Nakamura will be awesome regardless of their spot on the card, but I think that's because the fans that are there, these hardcore fans, are already super into AJ and Nakamura. I think these same fans are into Charlotte and Asuka, but that will depend on where they are on the card.

"Sometimes when your fifteen-minute match gets cut to nine minutes, that's not your only problem. Sometimes you go out there and the fans have already seen all of the big stars they wanted to see, and now they're waiting for the main event, but instead here's the *SmackDown* Women's Championship Match. If it hasn't become the focus of *SmackDown* TV, that's an issue. If there isn't a good story leading into it, that can lead to a negative perception of the match. All of those things go into play when talking about a match that's at that level of the show."

As for the persistent internet rumors of Undertaker coming out of retirement to face John Cena, even though the Dead Man did not appear at the *Rumble* as so many expected, Bryan hopes to see him back in the ring in New Orleans. "I will not believe he's retired until a *WrestleMania* goes by that he's not on. If we get to two *WrestleMania*s in a row that he's not on, then I'll think he's retired, or if he gives a Hall of Fame speech, then I'll think he's retired. There's something about wrestling that once it's in your blood, if you love it, it's hard to not come back, especially if you're given the opportunity to come back on a grand stage like *WrestleMania*. The allure of coming back for Undertaker is one: a really good pay day; two: what we do is a lot of fun, and if you love doing it, it's hard to say no.

"The only guy who insists he's not coming back is Shawn Michaels. In 2014, when I ended up in *WrestleMania XXX*, I thought, 'Okay, Shawn had screwed me at *Hell in a Cell*, so maybe there's this chance where we could do something at *WrestleMania*, like teacher versus student type thing. But when we had found out the finish for *Hell in a Cell*, Shawn was like, 'This is stupid, this just puts all the heat on me, and I'm not coming back.' I was like, 'If you did come back, just think of this.' And he was like, 'No, I'm not coming back.' I was like, 'Okay, but I'm going to convince you to come back.' No. Not coming back. So if Cena called out Shawn, I'd say, it's never happening. But Undertaker? I'm not surprised."

CHAPTER 19
Walk with Elias

FEBRUARY 12, 2018: *MONDAY NIGHT RAW*

Elias sits in the middle of the ring, strumming his guitar while holding the crowd with his every word. "I have one question for everybody here tonight. Who wants to walk with Elias?" he asks as the crowd erupts. "I gotta say, for San Jose, that was . . . pathetic." Elias then turns the crowd from cheers to jeers, like the natural antagonist he is. "The best thing about this city is the fact that it's an hour away from a real city, like San Francisco. Who am I kidding, every city in California is a toxic dump. Now do I need to remind you that I'm the man who defeated John Cena and Braun Strowman in the same place at the same time, which makes me the odds on favorite to win the Elimination Chamber. Which I will. And then I will go on *WrestleMania*. And it is at *WrestleMania* that the entire world will know what everyone here knows, that WWE stands for . . ."

The crowd screams back, "Walk with Elias!"

"I said WWE stands for . . ."

"Walk with Elias!" the crowd once again shoots back, even louder. Elias smirks as he responds, "I like the sound of that. You know what else I like the sound of? My own voice." Elias once again begins strumming his guitar as he sings, "I'm going to douse your dreams in gasoline and watch it go up in flames." Elias continues to play when the announcer interrupts.

"Ladies and gentleman, Braun Strowman."

Elias looks to the ramp when Strowman emerges playing a huge bass guitar so hard, the strings break off.

"Well, Elias says he's gonna win, but we all know that ain't true," Strowman sings. "You look at me, boy, when I'm singing, cause I'm not finished with you. You may not know it, you may not realize, but when this song's over, you're gonna get these hands!"

The two eventually battle inside the ring before Braun grabs his bass guitar and smashes it across Elias's back.

"It's very easy, everybody wants to be me. Everybody wants to be the guy out there with the spotlight on him, playing the guitar and entertaining the crowd," laughed Elias about the now classic segment. "Braun is no different. He wanted to do my thing, but it just so happens that he's a giant, so he found a giant guitar, sitting on a giant stool, and he smashed the giant thing over my back. I always wanted to know what that would feel like — to get hit with a bass guitar — so I finally got to check that off my bucket list."

This was just the latest in show-stealing segments from Elias who in under a year, since being called up from NXT, has quickly emerged as one of the most entertaining performers on the entire WWE roster, thanks to his combination of showmanship and in-ring skills, not to mention his ability to get under the skin of both fans and opponents with his hilarious and surprisingly catchy song lyrics.

"I think with a lot of people, there are big expectations when they get called up from NXT, but with me, I don't think there were these same expectations," says Elias, who debuted on *Raw* the night after *WrestleMania 33*. "There were a lot of unknowns, to be honest. But

when they finally got to see me and see what I was doing on *NXT Live* events, and I started playing the guitar on WWE television, the WWE Universe saw a side of me that they'd never seen before. It's really just me being myself, and being as true to myself as I can be every step of the way."

And while NXT fans might not have expected Elias to hit big on *Raw*, behind the scenes, everyone from the creative team to Triple H thought they had something special. "In talking with Triple H, he felt Elias was going to be a bigger star on *Raw* than in NXT," says Koskey. "If you look at it, the NXT audience knows the guys from the indies and from Japan, so the crowd gets excited to see those guys do their thing in NXT. With Elias, he's fine in the ring, but it's not like he's a technical marvel like a Sami Zayn or Daniel Bryan. So his gimmick was overlooked in NXT, but when he got up to *Raw*, he was able to do a lot more fun stuff that didn't involve simply having wrestling matches. It opened up the door for him to have some moments and connect with the crowd, and now he's one of the freshest parts of the show. Elias is great. He's always trying to push the envelope, and he's very hands-on with his character and working with the creative team on his songs and things like that."

Announcer Corey Graves agrees. "I think the whole presentation has been different on *Raw* than it was on NXT," says Graves, who has watched Elias grow from "The Drifter" he was billed as in NXT to the Superstar now showcased on Monday nights. "Sometimes when you get the right coat of paint on a certain talent, it's a vehicle for them to succeed in, and he's blowing the doors off. He took the opportunity and he's making the most of it. He's very, very entertaining, and he's one of those guys who is fun to boo and fun to dislike, and it's fun to watch him get beat up, and that's the base of what this business is. I think he's been doing a fantastic job since coming to *Raw*."

And that includes the bass beatdown by Braun, a moment that was conceived by Vince McMahon himself. "We're in the process of trying to develop Braun's character in a way where he's not just a monster," says Koskey. "You can always flip that switch and turn him back into that monster flipping things over, but we're trying to create a more well-rounded character, so you knew Braun was eventually going to get his hands on Elias. What type of fun can we have while they're out there to show Braun's funny side, his human side? Just flipping over stuff will always be fun, but we want Braun to have some more dimensions than just that. Bringing out the bass turned out to be a lot of fun. Elias is so good at getting the crowd to hate him. He's such an old-school villain who you want to see get beat up, and that night, adding Braun and that giant bass guitar was the perfect storm."

But Elias didn't become a Superstar overnight. Elias actually tried out multiple times to be signed to WWE development, only to be turned away after each audition. "I had done three paid tryouts, trying to get to WWE. I paid money, flew out to Florida, put myself in a hotel, and then tried out, but I got told no every single time," says Elias. "And then I did a tryout later on, where I was invited by William Regal. I did that tryout, and then a few months later, I was an extra on *WWE*

Raw, and William Regal told me that hiring was coming up and he would put in a good word for me, and that was the case."

Elias, who had been wrestling in the independents under the name Heavy Metal Jesus (complete with the rocker look, but no musical instruments), has actually been playing the guitar since he was 15, when he was obsessed with Eric Clapton. "I would listen to him day and night. I would even fall asleep listening to Eric Clapton, so my dad took notice of this, and for Christmas that year, he got me my first guitar," says Elias. "I tried to learn how to play Eric Clapton songs, then from there, I learned how to play other songs on the guitar, and then eventually created my own stuff. When I got into wrestling, it was never my intention to have a guitar with me or anything like that. In fact, even when I started the gimmick, I was pretty sure I'd only have the guitar during backstage promos, but never did I envision I'd be performing in front of the world, playing songs and playing the guitar in the middle of the ring."

It was Dusty Rhodes who first encouraged Elias to play in the ring during his stint in NXT. "Dusty was so fantastic, and he would give us creative freedom to try anything and everything we wanted, whether it was good or not," says Elias. "One of those times, I showed up with my guitar and I started telling a story while strumming some chords, and he took a real liking to it. I basically took it from that very first presentation class with Dusty Rhodes to where it is today, where I come up with these songs as I travel from city to city. I might be falling asleep one night, and a lyric will pop up in my head. It all depends on where I'm at in my day, where I'm at with my life, how I'm feeling, and what I want to get across to the audience that night."

And while Elias would love to add in the Heavy Metal Jesus gimmick to his brand, he doesn't see WWE agreeing to the name. "WWE is probably going to shy away from the Jesus name," he says with a laugh. "I love that name, and I remember when I got to NXT, I tried that name out really early on, but they shut that down."

One thing WWE didn't shut down was Elias's huge push at *Raw 25*,

where the new star was not only featured in a segment with Chris Jericho but also in the ring with John Cena and Jimmy Fallon. "I definitely have taken note of that moment, but I'm not one to sit back and go, 'Okay, now I've arrived,' or anything like that," Elias explains. "We've got *WrestleMania* coming up, and what I do there is extremely important to me. I definitely can't say whether or not I've arrived, that's for other people to decide, but I've got my own plans."

Could these plans include newly announced Hall of Famer Jeff Jarrett, a performer also notorious for smacking opponents with his guitar? "I don't even know if Jeff Jarrett plays the guitar. I know he could smack people with it, but I wonder if he can actually play," says Elias. "I wasn't given too many guidelines on how to hit people with my guitar, but it would be fun to see Jeff come down to the ring and see what happens. When it comes to *WrestleMania*, just give me the stage and let me do my thing. If I mix it up with John Cena or Chris Jericho or Braun Strowman or Finn Bálor . . . whoever it may be, I'll figure that out later. Just get me to the stage.

"Even when I was turned away and told I wasn't wanted, I never gave up. I always saw myself getting to WWE and eventually to *WrestleMania*. I didn't know how or when, but I believed in myself and I believed that one day I'd be in that ring."

CHAPTER 20
The Injury Bug Bites

FEBRUARY 14, 2018: WWE HEADQUARTERS,
STAMFORD, CONNECTICUT

Injuries are playing havoc with the proposed *WrestleMania 34* card. A rash of injuries has had a domino effect on several matches that were in the works. Dean Ambrose is out after having surgery on his triceps, and he won't return in time for the show. That cuts the proposed Shield breakup and Ambrose versus Rollins match Creative had hoped to highlight in New Orleans. In addition, Jason Jordan is out with a neck injury, putting a stop to the Jordan versus Kurt Angle match that was also planned. Add to that an injury to Kane that will prevent the Kane/Finn Bálor Demon versus Demon rivalry Creative had in the works, not to mention a foot injury sidelining Samoa Joe, and less than two months to the show, the card is in chaos. "Injuries have really caused the card to be reshuffled," said Ed Koskey. "It's like dominoes. You knock one over and the whole card can start tumbling down. We get injury reports from Talent Relations, and that helps us break everything down. We have a great Talent Relations department that keeps us up-to-date on people's medical conditions and their clearance dates and what the prognosis is. You get those updates and roll with the punches as best you can."

One of the main things Koskey and the creative writing team is attempting to pin down is Undertaker's status. Despite rumors of his return, Koskey says the dream match against John Cena is still not locked in. "It's not one hundred percent certain that he is coming back. Don't believe everything you read online," says Koskey. "When you start looking at the card and think about what you'd like to do at *WrestleMania*, you start floating the idea of, well, is Undertaker available? I think it also comes from *Raw 25*. We knew Taker was going to make an appearance, so we starting floating the idea around, is he available? How is he feeling? You kind of get the ball rolling there and see if it's something we can do. Right now, it's not one hundred percent official, but we're standing by and we should have official word pretty soon."

"That seems to be the old wrestling adage . . . you're only retired until your next big match," adds Brian James. "If that's the case, he has earned the respect to do whatever he wants to do for forever and a day in this business, but that said, personally as a fan — and I've been a lifelong fan of his — I thought it was a perfect ending to the tale of Undertaker. You hate to see a perfect ending to a story and then they tack something on and it's not quite as good, but knowing him, he wouldn't come back unless he believed he was able to top what happened last year."

Koskey is planning for 18 segments across the show, including the introduction of Hall of Famers, possible musical acts, and actual matches. "We'll be going off the air after midnight, which is what we did last year," he explained. "Nothing is locked in, and that's everything down on paper. Some matches will get truncated into triple threats or Fatal 4-Ways or some different elements. It has grown into a giant show, but we will be paring it down. We want to make it a great show, getting as many performers on the card as possible while at the same

time making it somewhat digestible, as opposed to just a marathon seven-hour setting."

But with six weeks left until the show, some of *Raw*'s top stars still don't have storylines, including The Miz, Braun Strowman, Finn Bálor, Seth Rollins, and Elias. "Right now, Braun might end up doing a match with The Miz, who is also doing amazing work. We thought the dynamic of those two could be very entertaining," said Koskey. "The question is, where does the Intercontinental Championship fall? If you put the title on Braun, how do you take it off of him eventually? There was also an idea that we've moved away from, but we thought about having Braun challenge Sheamus and Cesaro for the tag team titles by himself. We were looking at it in terms of doing something that had never been done before, and Braun is big enough to be tag team champion on his own, but we decided against it. A lot of storylines were changed because of the Jordan injury, and right now Braun looks like he's going after Miz's championship, but it's still a fluid situation.

"Elias is another guy we're trying to place. We're not sure if

we're going to use him in a match or if we want him to do a special *WrestleMania* musical performance or something like that, where he can get his own spotlight. He has stepped up tremendously in the past nine months. Who knows, after what has been happening between Braun and Elias, maybe that conflict continues through *WrestleMania*. We're still trying to figure out where all the pieces fit with a lot of guys. We may end up doing Seth versus Finn, or we may kind of shuffle some stuff around with Miz. Finn, Miz, Seth, Braun, and Elias . . . these guys are the most malleable part of the card right now as we try to find the best matches and storylines. But there are a couple of options for Finn, but in whatever we do, we want to make sure Finn brings out the Demon in New Orleans, because that entrance alone would be worth the price of admission."

One of the best parts of *Raw* this past year has been The Bar, and Koskey says that their challengers could come in a new team formed through the Matt Hardy/Bray Wyatt rivalry. "That's the plan. Matt and Bray going to Matt's compound and doing 'Eternal Deletion' or 'Woken World' or whatever we end up calling it," he said. "We're going to have Matt and Bray at the Hardy house, and maybe we end up with Bray seeing the light and Matt and Bray becoming a team. That's definitely a possibility of them challenging The Bar, but it all depends on when we can get all the footage shot from the Hardy Compound. We're also hoping to get Brother Nero back, but it all depends on how his shoulder heals."

Another big match being planned is Ronda Rousey and a mystery partner versus Triple H and Stephanie McMahon. With Rousey's inclusion in the Four Horsewomen of MMA, original rumors looked to have a Four-on-Four Match against WWE's own version of the Four Horsewomen, or a match that would feature Rousey versus Charlotte as the leaders of each respective group. But for her first match, "we want to put her in a protected spot, in terms of presenting her in the best way," Koskey says. "Hunter and Stephanie are two people she's very familiar and friendly with, so to have her out there with two people

who can make her feel comfortable is important. And Hunter is fantastic in terms of putting matches together. With that being said, the tag match gives her the best showcase in a high-profile match. At the same time, it's important to have her in the tag match as opposed to starting her off against someone like Charlotte because you don't want Ronda to come in and just start blowing through all of the main-roster talent. Having her start out against Hunter and Stephanie seemed like the best thing to do for Ronda, the show, and for everybody.

"We did that thing a couple of years ago with Rock and Ronda, but that doesn't look like it could happen due to Rock's schedule," continues Koskey. Vince McMahon reached out to The Rock, but the two could not come to agreement due to The Rock's trip to China during *Mania* weekend. "Kurt is in the discussion to be her partner now, especially since his match against Jason Jordan isn't happening. John Cena was floated as an option as well. As the dominos were falling, we even thought Braun Strowman and Ronda, but we felt that might be a little too gimmicky for Ronda's first match. We were aiming for more legitimacy in her match as opposed to Braun being the outlandish Monster Among Men."

But what about a surprise return of Samoa Joe? "You don't want to get burned making plans where they tell you, don't worry, he'll be back, but then what if he's not?" says Koskey. "It's one of those things where, when we get closer, maybe we can shift some things around, but you just want to make sure he'll be ready. When we get closer to Joe getting cleared, we'll re-evaluate. It's just the worst timing for Joe. We'll see where he's at and hopefully make the most out of his return. After *SummerSlam*, we were going to do a story with Joe and Cena, and then Joe tweaked his knee. Then the night he got hurt this year, he was cutting a promo about John Cena. We just need to stop planning to do matches between Samoa Joe and John Cena for the good of Joe's health."

CHAPTER 21
Five Feet of Fury

FEBRUARY 25, 2018: *ELIMINATION CHAMBER*

The *Elimination Chamber* pay-per-view sets three huge *WrestleMania* storylines in motion. Roman Reigns wins the men's Chamber Match to officially become the number one contender for Brock Lesnar's Universal Championship. Ronda Rousey not only signs her WWE contract, she puts Triple H through a table, setting up her debut in New Orleans. And, finally, Alexa Bliss successfully defends her *Raw* Women's Championship, setting her up for a title match at *Mania* against Nia Jax. In the coming month, Bliss's storyline would see her flip from Jax's best friend to a backstabbing mean girl, igniting one of the more personal rivalries on the card.

When Bliss showed up to the T-Mobile Arena the day of the *Elimination Chamber*, she was shocked at the size and intimidation factor of the chamber structure itself. "It was very intimidating and very scary," says Bliss, a former Division 1 cheerleader and competitive bodybuilder who now finds herself at the forefront of the Women's Evolution. "Once we actually stepped inside the chamber, it was a different setup than we initially thought it would be. It was different than the chambers in the past, so all of the ideas we went in with had to go out the window. It was scary but it was a lot of fun at the same time.

"This was the first-ever Women's Elimination Chamber Match, and any time it's the first for anything, we want to make sure we take our time and do it right. We're always trying to step up our game when it comes to the Women's Evolution. So we wanted to make sure we delivered."

And to Bliss, delivering included her not only scurrying up the cage but taking a leap of faith and hitting a Twisted Bliss from the top of a pod. "I was so afraid of it," admits Bliss. "I wasn't able to practice the move beforehand — it was more of a *do it while you're out there* kind of thing."

The victory means that Bliss is entering *WrestleMania* as the *Raw* Women's Champion, fulfilling one of the her goals after being moved from *SmackDown* in 2017. "The first *WrestleMania* I ever had, I walked in as *SmackDown*'s Women's Champion, and it was amazing," says Bliss. "Now I'm walking into my second *WrestleMania* as the *Raw* Women's Champion. I can't wait until *WrestleMania*. Last year I had the most amazing feeling during my entrance, and I can't wait to feel it this year."

Bliss's battle against Nia Jax is something both women are looking forward to — the women might trade strikes on-screen, but off-screen, they remain best friends. "You're able to see it in storylines, on *Total Divas*, and in real life: we ride together, we hang out together all the time, and we listen to each other," says Bliss. "But as the storyline goes, we're not best friends anymore, so it's going to be very interesting because it's more of a personal match. It's not just a normal championship match where all the focus is on the moves. This match will have a lot of emotion."

When Nia Jax first tried out for NXT, Bliss was working the training session, and during the lunch break, Jax walked up to Bliss and the two started talking. "We're both smart alecks, so it's fun," laughs Bliss. "We clicked instantly and we've been best friends ever since. We do

karaoke, we go to Starbucks multiple times per day. We have the same type of schedule and same type of mentality. You have to travel with someone you mesh with and who has the same values. Some people like to be up at 6 a.m. and go to the gym — we don't."

The mean-girl storyline involves both bullying and body shaming, two subjects that Jax takes personally. "I think it's something that not only young girls but also young boys — and even grown women and grown men — can relate to," says Jax. "We're dealing with bullying and being made fun of for your looks. I feel like this is great for young kids to see because they can think, 'Look at her, she's going to face her bully and she has confidence in who she is.' I know I'm a constant work in progress, but everybody should love who they are in that moment. I think this is a great storyline for everybody to see play out. From the bullying to the body shaming, and just like dealing with any type of adversity in life, you have to deal with it head-on and have the confidence to overcome it.

"I really like where we've gone with the story. There's shock value to it, like, 'I can't believe they said that about her,' but I'm like, 'Great, do it, let's make this as real as possible.' This is what people go through. Don't sugarcoat it. I want to make this story relatable to the people. No matter who you are, no matter where you're from, everybody goes through something like this."

Jax remembers instances of bullying in her teen years, by not only other students, but from parents of rival schools. "In junior high, I was playing basketball against one of our local teams and I was dominating the whole game," says Jax. "But then one of the fathers from the other team started shouting about my size. 'It's not fair. Look at her. She's just a big fat girl!' He didn't realize that my dad, my big Samoan father, was sitting a few feet away from him. As I was running down the court, I saw my dad fly to the top of the bleachers and real-life Superman punch him and Samoan drop him. Not something I condone, but what are you going to do? He was defending his daughter's honor."

And while Bliss also sees the importance of the storyline, she explains how playing the role of the bully on *Raw* is a complete 180 from her character in *NXT*. "When I was a good guy, it just wasn't translating," says Bliss. "I felt like I was in a constant struggle against myself. The character I was portraying in *NXT* was an extension of myself and it was who I thought my character should be, but ever since I turned into a bad guy and I've been able to play this villain role, it's been so much more fun. There's just so much more freedom in it, and it's just something I genuinely enjoy doing."

In order to transform into the villain role, Bliss also had to go through an extreme makeover. "I was able to establish the character with Blake and Murphy in *NXT* because I didn't have to focus on matches," says Bliss. "I was a valet, so I got to focus one hundred percent on the character, so that helped me tremendously. I remember when I started with Blake and Murphy, it was on a Thursday morning after an *NXT TakeOver*. We left the arena at midnight and I had blue hair and a blue outfit. I show up to Full Sail the next morning and Michael Hayes asks, 'Where is your red hair?' I was like, 'What? Nobody told

me I had to have red hair." And he said, 'Can it be red in the next five hours?' So my hair changed, my outfit changed, and I knew my personality had to change. If I wasn't going to run with this new character, I wasn't going to succeed with it."

Heading into *WrestleMania*, Bliss says the key is to constantly keep her character evolving. "Nowadays, with social media and television and movies, everyone's attention span is so short," she says. "You have to keep evolving and changing and keep things fresh and interesting. For me, it was as simple as going from having blue hair to red hair. I needed that refresher. I needed that change. Same thing with the gray in my hair now, it signals the change in my character. I've gone from being this bratty person to being a chicken to being bratty again to a downright mean girl. There are so many dynamics that go into making a memorable character: What degree of that character are you today? When am I going to show another side? How do I show off a different dimension? These are all things I constantly think about. I always watch people and I figure out what about them irritates me, then I use that in the ring. If it's going to irritate me, it's going to irritate someone else."

Bliss and Jax plan to work out the match once they get to New Orleans, but both see it as one of the most passionate, personality-based matches on the card. "The good thing about Alexa and me is no matter what is going down inside the ring, we have trust in each other. She knows what I do, I know what she does, and hopefully we can come together to create an epic story."

The story means Jax will even show off a new *WrestleMania* outfit. "I have gear that's a little bit out of my comfort zone," says Jax. "Nobody ever likes my gear, and it's funny because I'm athletic, so I want gear that's going to be comfortable and I want to make sure I can do certain moves without having to worry about something falling out. That's why I have the gear that I have. For *WrestleMania*, I do have special gear. It's going to be a little different than what people are used to seeing me in, so I'm very excited, but at the same time, I'm nervous to see what people will think.

"No matter what, I'm always going to have the butterflies and the anxiety, so I'm used to it. I actually love that stuff. I love the butterflies. I love the nerves. It gives me motivation to go in and just do better. I don't ever want to lose that feeling, I don't ever want to lose those nerves before I walk out, whether it's five hundred people or seventy thousand people. Having those nerves means I'm about to do something special."

CHAPTER 22
The Right Angle

FEBRUARY 26, 2018: *MONDAY NIGHT RAW*

Roman Reigns is about to deliver the best promo of his career. After winning the Elimination Chamber the night before, WWE announced a face-off between Reigns and Lesnar for Monday night. The creative plans surrounding *WrestleMania*'s main event call for walking the fine line between shoot and storyline. Playing off the reality of both Brock Lesnar's and Paul Heyman's soon-to-be expiring contracts and Lesnar's photo with UFC President Dana White being released on social media during the pay-per-view, Reigns plays to the fans' passion for WWE by calling out Lesnar for being a part-timer who wants to return to UFC. After a year that saw him battle Braun Strowman, beat John Cena, reunite with The Shield, not win the Royal Rumble, and win the Elimination Chamber, it's his put-downs of Lesnar and calling the Universal champ a "bitch" that has the WWE Universe finally by his side (at least for this night).

"I'm a man of my word," Reigns tells the crowd. "I said I was going to win the Elimination Chamber, and I did. So when I say I'm going to *WrestleMania* and I can beat Brock Lesnar, I'm telling the truth. The truth . . . truth is a funny word, you know. I don't know why I'm covering for this guy. You guys want to know the truth? They're not going to like it back there, but I'm going to say it anyway, Brock Lesnar is not here tonight. Up until about thirty minutes ago, I thought Brock was going to be here, but something happened and he didn't show. And nobody will say this back there, but I'm going to say it: Brock Lesnar is an entitled piece of crap who hides behind his contract. Think about it, y'all. Think about it. We are six weeks away from *WrestleMania* and the Universal Champion is not here today. We were in Vegas last night, Brock was in Vegas, but he wasn't at the Elimination Chamber. Guess where he was. He was running around the Strip taking pictures with Dana White and the UFC on social media. You want to know why? Because he doesn't respect me, he doesn't respect any of you, and he doesn't respect anybody in that locker room. And I'm sick of it. We're all sick of it. They all know it back there. We all know it. Every single week, me and those boys run across this road and we bust our ass. And Brock just shows up whenever he wants to, whenever the money is right and the city is right. But we don't care. It doesn't matter how many people show up or how big the town is, I'll be there because I said I'll be there. And Brock and Paul, don't worry, they're going to come out here and say, 'We're businessmen.' Well, guess what? I was born in this business. My family and my bloodline is this business, and I was taught at an early age that there is a fine line between business and respect. And I'll say this right now, I don't respect Brock Lesnar. And I damn sure don't fear that bitch.

"I think I've said enough now. I'm going to go and head to the back and take my ass-chewing like a man, because unlike some people, I actually care and respect this place." Mic drop.

But it's not the only major development on *Raw*. After the chaotic confrontation between Rousey, Angle, Stephanie McMahon, and Triple H at *Elimination Chamber* (including Stephanie slapping Rousey across the face), Rousey demands an apology from the power couple. But after McMahon apologizes to Rousey, Triple H cheap-shots Angle, signaling the beginning of the four competitors' *WrestleMania* storyline that would eventually lead to a match between the team of Rousey and Angle against Triple H and Stephanie.

"Triple H came to me and asked me what I thought, and I said I thought it would be great," says Angle. "To get in the ring with Triple H and partner up with Ronda, that's an excellent opportunity, and anyone in the business would take that — anybody. You're not the main event, you're not in the championship match, but you're a feature match, you're a headline match. That's what we all want. That's what we're all looking for. We're going to have an important place on the card, and hopefully we deliver.

"At first, I was told I was going to work with Jason Jordan at *Mania*, and I was really looking forward to getting in the ring with him. We were really going to continue to bring out more of Jason's personality through the storyline. Vince thought it would be a good idea to push the storyline, and we were pleasantly surprised at the backlash that he got. We heard everything from 'Jason sucks' to 'the storyline sucks,' and it wasn't just heat, this was real heat. You don't get that very often. They hated his guts, and it was great. This was going to lead to me eventually wrestling him at *WrestleMania*, but because of the injury, we had to change things up. I will tell you this, though: right now, Jason Jordan is one of the top five performers in the business. He is very much overlooked in his ability. If you go back and watch his matches, you'll see what I'm talking about. After *WrestleMania*, we're going to pick back up with the storyline and I'm really looking forward to getting in the ring with him."

But before Angle can lock up with Jordan, there is the immediate business with Triple H and Stephanie he needs to deal with. This plays off the old Attitude Era days between the three, a time Angle calls "a lot of fun," remembering an embarrassing moment where Angle needed to kiss Stephanie in front of Vince. "I had to kiss Stephanie, which was very weird because her dad was directing the shot," Angle

remembers with a laugh. "I had her dad three feet away while I'm kissing his daughter. When we were done, Stephanie told me I kiss like a fish, and I was like, 'What do you want? Your dad was sitting there watching.'

"I always wanted a match with Triple H after our original storyline. When I was main-eventing with Triple H, I was really new to the business, so I didn't know a lot, I didn't have a lot of experience, and he carried me a lot in those matches. Now that I have a lot of experience, I'd like to have another match with Triple H. It's a little later than I expected, but I'm glad I'm able to do it at *WrestleMania*."

WrestleMania will be Angle's third match after returning to WWE in 2017. In his first match, at *TLC*, Angle joined The Shield in what turned out to be a surreal moment for everyone involved. "Kurt hadn't been in WWE for eleven years, and he hadn't wrestled a match in any capacity for some time," says Seth Rollins. "He got the call just a few days before the match, so he wasn't physically or mentally prepared, but at the same time, Kurt Angle is also an elite-level competitor, and he has been for most of his adult life. He was able to step in and fill in better than anyone could've ever expected, especially in a match like that: five-on-three, anything goes. It was awesome to see and awesome to be a part of. For Ambrose and I, it was a cool experience to team up with Kurt. It was something neither one of us ever expected to do. And also to have him in Shield gear and have him come down with our entrance — it was definitely a unique experience for us, for Kurt, and for the WWE Universe."

"It was ridiculous," adds Dean Ambrose. "I just kept laughing and going, 'This is ridiculous!' I didn't realize he was going to be wearing the Shield gear. I walked past his change room and I saw him pulling his pants up and he was already wearing the attack vest, and I knew right then this was going to be hilarious. We had to do our entrance through the crowd, so we went up to the top of the arena, and they always try to hide us in some broom closet before we go out. We were up in some tiny storage area and we're used to being in a closet with Roman, but for some reason, we're stuck in a closet with Kurt Angle. It was so surreal. I just kept laughing at the situation."

"I never stopped wrestling after I left WWE," explains Angle. "I went to TNA, and I've had matches with Cody Rhodes, Alberto Del Rio, and Rey Mysterio — big names who I trust, to keep me sharp. But after not having a match for six or seven months, it was nice that there were seven of us in the match. I had an injury while I was training for my comeback. I had pulled a muscle in my leg and it haunted me for both *TLC* and *Survivor Series*, so I really couldn't do a lot. I'm just really happy now, heading into *WrestleMania*, I'm finally healthy again."

And heading into New Orleans, Angle can't help but see a little of himself in his partner, Ronda Rousey. "Not just because of the Olympics and what kind of athlete she was in MMA, but because of how quickly she's picking everything up. I trained for three days before I had my first match. I wouldn't say Ronda is *that* quick, but she is picking things up quickly. Ronda likes to control the situation. She's very aggressive, but you have to be very passive in WWE — you have to allow your opponent to throw you around — but her instincts tell her to not let that happen. She also tends to force her throws, not allowing her opponent to jump with her. She can launch them without any warning, but when you throw your opponent, you have to jump together so that your opponent lands safely. It has taken Ronda a little bit of time to learn not to just launch her opponent, but she's adjusting pretty fast.

"The biggest difference: Ronda's first match is going to be *WrestleMania*. That's a big difference between a small show with three hundred people, where if you mess up, you don't need to worry because nobody will remember, and *WrestleMania*, where the whole world is watching. So there are a lot of similarities, but Ronda is going to have to carry her own weight at *WrestleMania*, and I think she can do it."

CHAPTER 23
Oh, You Didn't Know!?!

MARCH 1, 2018: WWE HEADQUARTERS,
STAMFORD, CONNECTICUT

As a member of D-Generation X, Brian James (aka Road Dogg) starred in some of the most infamous moments of WWE's famed Attitude Era. From the WCW invasion (complete with camouflage and armored vehicle) to arguably the catchiest entrance phrase in sports-entertainment history (Oh, you didn't know? Your ass better call somebody!), the d-o-double-g character never fell flat when it came to creative direction. "Back in the Attitude Era, [head writer] Vince Russo wrote Triple H and I into some interesting situations," James says. "And back in the DX days, we would come up with some funny ideas and ways to get out of those situations."

So when James finally hung up his boots and retired from in-ring competition, it came as no surprise that his old friend and D-Generation X running mate, Triple H, proposed a new career. "Hunter called me and asked, 'Hey, would you be interested in working in the creative side of our business?' We always worked well together, so I was like, 'Heck yeah, I'm interested.' After a couple of failed attempts to get me hired, Vince finally said yes, and I became a producer behind the scenes." James was hired in October 2011 in his new role to help put matches together. "Putting matches together was easy to me, so then Hunter wanted to see if I could help out with some of the creative writing. It was kind of a whirlwind, and it's still a whirlwind as I learn on the job. I'm not a writer, but there are television writers on my team and we write the show together. I come up with a lot of the creative, then they help me write it and format the structure of the show. It's been a journey. I've been working here almost six years, and here I am, the Vice President of *SmackDown* Creative Writing."

James reflected on his career from inside his office at WWE headquarters. He and his staff were busy trying to finalize the *SmackDown* side of the show, with *WrestleMania* being only 38 days away. His first order of business? Find a place on the card for The Usos. "The Usos will definitely be on the card. Not the kickoff — The Usos will be on the *WrestleMania* main show," James says emphatically. "I just found out about three weeks ago that they have been here nine years and have never been on the actual show. When I found that out, that became the first thing on my agenda with Vince. I wanted to make that known and I wanted to correct that mistake, and I do feel like it's a mistake. If there is ever a year where they deserve to be on the show, it's this year. The year 2017 was the year of the Usos. They have raised the bar in tag team matches as far as performance goes, as far as their promos. They're Pensacola boys; I grew up with their dad, so I couldn't be more proud of those guys. I've made it my goal to not only put them on the show but also to give them a really cool match. It will be The Usos versus The New Day versus The Bludgeon Brothers in a triple threat for the *SmackDown* Tag Team Championships."

But while James was sure of the direction of the tag team scene, one thing he still hadn't figured out is John Cena's place in *WrestleMania*. Rumors initially had Cena fighting Undertaker, with the Dead Man coming out of retirement, but then *Sports Illustrated* wrote a story saying Undertaker wasn't going to be available for the event, and Rey

Mysterio could be stepping in his place to take on Cena. "Truth be told, it's above my pay grade to know whether or not Taker is in," admits James. "I heard he was out, but I also know that Rey Mysterio was talked to, so there is some feeling out going on right now, but we still have a month to go. I'm trying to see what Taker's health status is and if he wants to do one more. I know John would love to have his match against Taker, so it looks like we're still waiting on the final verdict. If there has been a decision made, I don't know about it yet, and that's not crazy or unheard of. I didn't know Ronda Rousey was going to show up at the *Royal Rumble* until I saw her walk out, so it's not crazy for them to keep things close to their vest and then surprise the world with it."

It just goes to show, despite James's Vice President role, the show is still run by Vince McMahon. Says James, "Sometimes I'll bring something to him that I think is great, and he'll say, 'Why would you do it this way? What if you did this?' And then I think, 'Why didn't I see it

that way?' It just reminds me of how much I have to learn as I sit under the proverbial learning tree in his office. And sometimes I disagree with him, but we can either meet in the middle or do it his way. He's a genius, and I'm not just saying that because he's my boss. He's a promotional and creative genius, and he proves it. But we take stuff up to him every day, and he's like, 'That's great. Good stuff, guys.' So it's give and take, and if you're willing to listen, you can learn a lot from him."

And since Vince has final say over the storylines, he gets to decide when, or if, the Chairman returns to the ring. With the Kevin Owens headbutt still lingering and Sami Zayn's and Owens's constant harassment of Shane McMahon, could we see a Vince and Shane tag team in New Orleans? It's something Owens wants (if he can't have a singles match against Vince, that is), but James isn't so sure. "Of course, Kevin wants Vince, because Kevin is smart," he laughs. "But I don't know if that would be wise from a creative standpoint. Vince is money when it comes to promos and strutting down to the ring, he's money every time. But him being in a singles match against Kevin, I don't know if that would be best for everybody. I would love to have Shane and Vince against Kevin and Sami for *Mania*, but we'll have to see how that plays out."

James said the original plan was for Shane to have a singles match against either Owens or Zayn, but things have transitioned to a tag match. "They'll definitely be in a match against Shane and somebody," he says. "We talked about Shane and Hunter. We've talked about all kinds of people being Shane's partner. As we get closer, we'll find out who that will be."

One man on the list of potential partners is Dolph Ziggler. "There was a completely different direction and storyline for Dolph, before he laid the United States Championship in the ring," says James of Ziggler's perplexing United States Championship reign. "There was a totally different direction we were going to go, but then we changed direction after he laid it down. So we brought him back for the *Rumble*, and we thought we'd start over from there. Dolph is great at what he does, he's one of the best in the ring that we've had in a long time. He's been on the edge of 'Am I going to stay, am I going to go,' and sometimes we get different Dolphs in there, depending on where his head is. I feel like he's in a good place now, I feel like we're going to give him some good stuff moving forward, and he definitely added a lot to the Six-Pack Challenge. He brings something special when he comes out to the ring, and the people know it. He's been around so long, he's established, and the crowd pops for him like a babyface anyway because he's such an established star. It's hard to turn him heel, so right now, he's more of a tweener. He comes out, and sometimes he does things that are perceived as a babyface, but then he does something heelish too. Right now, there are only a few guys who can get away with doing that. Randy Orton is another one. Dolph can do that because he's a good-looking guy you want to punch in the face, but he might just steal your girlfriend while you're at it. We're definitely looking for a match for him at *Mania*, and he's being tossed around as Shane's partner. We just need to see how the next four weeks play out before we make a decision on Dolph or Shane."

One thing James knows for sure, though, is the *Mania* match he's most anticipating: AJ Styles versus Shinsuke Nakamura. "To be quite honest, this is the match all of the hardcore fans, all of the internet fans want to see," says James. "They always say how we don't listen to them — but we listen and they got their match. Don't get me wrong, though, we didn't just do it to please them: we think it's the right thing to do and it'll be a great match. This is a dream match, and AJ has been fighting hard to get this match. Shinsuke has been a pleasure to work with since he arrived. He has a great attitude, a great work ethic, and he just wants to do what you ask him to do. But he was really excited to get this match at *Mania*. The people wanted it. AJ wanted it. It's a bonus for everybody, and they're going to get to see it at *Mania*."

As for the final weeks before *WrestleMania*, James expects a lot of late nights as they finalize all of the storylines heading into the big show. "Here's the truth of it: we're all going to be burning the candle from both ends, especially when we get to New Orleans," he says. "In April, we go from the go-home shows on *Raw* and *SmackDown* straight to New Orleans, and we will meet with Vince multiple times every day, and we will go over everything from the match order to the music order to the announcers to the musical acts to rehearsals. It's the craziest, busiest week of the year, for sure, but it's so rewarding when you're standing there in Gorilla and you watch all your hard work, all those late nights, come to fruition in front of your eyes. You're watching the show, and all you can think is 'How in the flip are we going to top that next year?' And then next year we do it again."

CHAPTER 24
Bálor Club
for Everyone

MARCH 5, 2018: *MONDAY NIGHT RAW*

Finn Bálor has a secret entrance planned for *WrestleMania*, and it has nothing to do with the Demon, a Voodoo Demon, or even a chain-saw. "I got a couple of tricks up my sleeve but no demon," says Bálor, whose cosplaying Demon King persona become a worldwide sensation. "Only four people know about my entrance right now, and that's Vince McMahon, Kevin Dunn, Triple H, and me. I can't reveal anything, but it's going to be very inclusive and a step in the right direction not only for WWE but for humanity."

And while Bálor wouldn't elaborate any further on his entrance, thanks to a change in creative plans, the Intercontinental Championship Match moved from The Miz defending his title against Braun Strowman to a triple threat featuring three of the top workhorses in WWE: The Miz, Finn Bálor, and Seth Rollins. "As a child watching WWE, I always watched the Intercontinental Title Matches," says Bálor. "It's always been a great title and it's always delivered great matches. Whether the champ was The Honky Tonk Man or Shawn Michaels or Randy

Savage, these are guys who, once the bell rang, you knew you were going to see something special, and to just be considered in the same vein is an honor. We want to go out and live up to the legacy of the great Intercontinental matches before us, and I'm hoping to walk out as the first-ever Irish Intercontinental Champion."

As for his opponents, Bálor couldn't think of two other competitors he'd rather be in the ring with in New Orleans. "The Miz is one of the most underrated Superstars in WWE history," says Bálor. "He's not only great at using his words to get under your skin, but when the bell rings, The Miz delivers. He has main-evented *WrestleMania* before against John Cena, he's done it all, and people still underestimate his skill in the ring. And then when you talk Seth Rollins, Seth and myself have a lot of history. The injury I suffered at *SummerSlam* was against Seth, and that took away seven months from the prime of my career. So there's a lot of respect as a competitor, but there's still some personal heat that we need to settle between ourselves. We both have this professional, competitive nature to be the best, and that helps us bring out the best in each other. There are a lot of dynamics going into the match, and it's going to make for an entertaining three-way.

"From a personal standpoint, it's the journey up to *WrestleMania* that has me wanting to steal the show. I've been in professional wrestling for eighteen years, but I'm going into my first *WrestleMania*. I narrowly missed out on *WrestleMania* last year due to injury. The bitter part about that is I was medically cleared by the doctors but only a week before the show, so it was a little late to try and find an opponent. I've watched the last three *WrestleMania*s from the stands, but this is the first time I'll ever be involved, so this is a huge moment for me. It's a career milestone. This is my chance to show the world that I belong in WWE and to prove it on the biggest platform possible, and that's *WrestleMania*."

WrestleMania will cap one of Bálor's most entertaining runs since he arrived from NXT. Bálor lasted almost an hour in the 2018 *Royal Rumble* (after entering the ring at number two) and hit a number of

memorable spots inside the Elimination Chamber. "It was my first *Royal Rumble* and it was a big opportunity," says Bálor. "It was a little bit of a surreal moment for me because growing up, I watched so many *Royal Rumbles*. It's always a match that everybody pays attention to, and whether you're a WWE fan or not, it gets people talking. So it was a huge honor to go in at number two. I knew I was going to have to put my working boots on, that this was going to be a long night, and I lasted inside the ring for fifty-seven minutes and thirty-six seconds. A lot of people congratulated me on my performance, but I was upset I didn't hit that hour mark. That's a number that's sought after by a lot of professionals. The match took a lot out of me, both physically and mentally. You go through a lot of emotions, especially when you're in there for almost an hour; I was beat up for a couple of days after the match, for sure.

"As for the Elimination Chamber — physically, the structure is huge. I wasn't expecting that. I've been in cage matches before, but I've never seen an Elimination Chamber or Hell in a Cell in person;

I've only seen them on TV. So I stepped into the Elimination Chamber before the show, and I just stood in there and tried to grasp how daunting it was. What was really interesting is that my peripheral vision was taken away. The chain-link wall almost acted like a mirror, and I felt like I couldn't interact with the WWE Universe, and it was definitely something that took a few minutes to get used to, not being able to see people's faces who are sitting ringside. I was pretty happy with my performance. Live to fight another day, and here I am, on the verge of making my first ever *WrestleMania* appearance."

All this after an online rumor suggested Vince McMahon didn't think Finn Bálor was "over" enough to be a featured Superstar. "I only hear from my friends what's going on online; I don't really pay attention to it," laughs Bálor. "I got a text from one of my buddies back home in Ireland, and he said, 'They're saying this about you.' I took it with a little bit of tongue-in-cheek and tried to stir the pot a little bit. If someone tells me it's raining outside, I'm going to walk outside to see if it's raining. I don't believe anything on the internet. If Vince McMahon believes something, he'll tell me to my face, so I don't worry about what the internet is saying for one second."

CHAPTER 25
I Don't Give a Damn 'Bout My Reputation

MARCH 7, 2018: THE PERFORMANCE CENTER

Known as "The Baddest Woman on the Planet," former UFC champion Ronda Rousey is arguably one of the most influential female athletes of her generation. So when the Olympian and box-office badass decided to pursue her lifelong dream of joining WWE, it wasn't a move she took lightly. "Deep down, I want to be the change I wish to see in the world," says Rousey, while taking a quick break from her training inside the WWE Performance Center in Orlando. "I think WWE is social commentary for the world, and to effect real social change, I feel this is the place to do it. I have a lot left in me to contribute, and I want to contribute. I can go live in a mansion off in the middle of nowhere and never show my face again, but that wouldn't make me happy. I feel like this is the most fulfilling path for me."

Rousey, who grew up a fan of "Rowdy" Roddy Piper, got the blessing of Piper's son to wear the Hall of Famer's trademark black leather jacket to the ring when she debuted after the first-ever Women's Royal Rumble, and she says she is now all-in on her WWE career. And if her countless hours of training in the Performance Center are any indication, she's about to take WWE by storm in the same way she rocked the UFC. "I started training for WWE in August of last year. It was actually for my bachelorette party," laughs Rousey as she explains how her WWE signing came about. "I really wanted a shot and I really wanted to try out, but I was too afraid of rejection. I didn't want to put myself out there and get shot down. So I didn't ask Triple H for a tryout or anything. I was like, 'I'm getting married and all my best friends are out in Orlando, I was wondering if for my bachelorette party we could train at the Performance Center all week, and then we're going to get a Cruise America and drive that home to Los Angeles.' That was a way to put my foot in the door in the most timid way possible. But, hey, it worked. I could've just called up and said, 'I want to try this out,' but I guess I was just too much of a wuss. It happened, and I wanted it to happen organically anyway, so this was the way it all fell together.

"After the greatest bachelorette party of all time, I was bit hard by the bug and asked my best friend Marina's fiancé, Roderick Strong, who is in NXT right now, if he knew anybody who would work with me out in L.A., and he recommended Brian Kendrick. The training was at Santino's [Santino Bros. Wrestling Academy], about two hours from where I lived, so for several months I would drive the two hours, train for two to three hours, then drive two hours back. It would end up being like seven hours just to get a few hours of training. It was very reminiscent of my early days in judo and MMA. When I first started judo, me and my mom would have to drive three hours during rush hour, then I would do the kids class and the adult class back to back, then we'd drive back home. Then when I started doing MMA, I would have to drive to the Valley twice a day, up the 405 in my Honda. So those long drives are really reminiscent of those early days where I was trying to learn a new skill from scratch, and I think that's what really brings out the best in me — not just being really motivated but being present. It's easy to become a master of something and just go through the motions because you know you can do things without thinking.

When you have to pick something up that's entirely new to you, it requires every fiber of your being to try to get something right and to try to understand something that you don't understand. Even though it was a grind, I was just happy. It wasn't like, 'Oh God I have to drive for hours to get to Santino's and back.' It was like, 'I have wrestling today!' It was just fun, and I didn't think I'd ever feel that again.

"After a while, I called and said, 'Hey, can I come to the Performance Centre just to train? You can totally shoot me down if you want to,' but they were happy to have me back. I was shy because of how much I sucked. I was like, 'I don't want everybody to see how bad I am,' but everybody was really cool and the coaches were really patient. The girls here have been helping me train, and they've been extremely generous with the miles on their bodies that they're giving me by taking falls from me. They have every right in the world to be apprehensive about training with me because everything I have been trained is to hurt people. I have habits to hurt people. It takes some bravery from them to trust me and to endure my learning curve. I couldn't have been more impressed not just by the coaches and the staff here but the other women here. I'm used to it being everyone out for themselves, with very, very few exceptions, like the Four Horsewomen, but that's why they are so special. It was me versus everyone all the time. As a swimmer, it was me versus everyone. In judo, me versus everyone. In fighting, me versus everyone. Then finally I come here and everyone is like, 'What can we do to make you as good as possible?' And I'm like, 'Wait a minute. This is all one big team as opposed to everyone having their own separate team?' It's good to have a group of people all solely focused on you. That has helped me improve a lot. This is the least lonely endeavor I've ever pursued."

For Rousey, the training at the Performance Center was different than her training for MMA and judo, describing it more as grueling than intense, but she is willing to put in whatever work necessary to make sure her *WrestleMania* debut earns the respect of the WWE Universe. "For judo and MMA, one of my old coaches would say that

training is like sex, if it takes longer than an hour and a half, you're not doing it right," laughs Rousey. "So training would be very intense for an hour and a half. Then I would take a break and do more training later. But because I don't need to worry so much about my body being one hundred percent recovered by the day I'm actually performing, I don't have to worry so much about preserving my body and making sure I'm at one hundred percent peak condition that day. Any disadvantage that you have, any ailment on your body, any ache is an advantage that your opponent has, whereas in WWE, it just has to be worth the trade-off. Is me being extra sore on the day of *WrestleMania* worth the extra time I spent learning those other things? It's a decision I have to weigh, as opposed to fighting, where there is no weighing it, you have to be one hundred percent physically at your best. That gives me the freedom to train a lot longer. If I was fighting, I would have to train for an hour and a half, then I'd have to eat so many ounces of this, then I rest for this many hours, then get up and eat this thing, then stretch at this time, then I'd have to train at this exact time because that's the time my fight is at, so I have to get my body used to being active at this time at night. Everything is so regimented, as opposed to 'Okay, we got a bunch of stuff to learn today, we have about six hours, so let's start some stuff.' It's all about improving and learning and not about, I used to call it, shaving the arm hairs. In swimming, I'd shave my arm hairs off because maybe that little bit of a drag would make a difference. I've been able to let go of the anxiety of having to keep track of all of the little details like that."

"There's a lot of adjusting to do," she continues when asked whether or not she has any doubts about her own ability in making the transition to WWE. "There are a lot of skills that carry over, but a lot that don't. The way that I throw people is with the intention to hurt them as much as possible, and the timing that I throw people is to be as unexpected as possible. So it has been interesting to take those skills that I already have and adjust them to have them apply in this environment. It's humbling knowing that I know nothing. There are some other skills that I have that can be extremely useful when applied correctly, but that's why I need the Performance Center and all of the coaches to show me how and where to apply those things. I have a bunch of ingredients to make a cake but no idea how to make a cake.

"I'm pretty sure I'm going to be learning and working up until the very last second of *WrestleMania*. If I had a whole year to prepare, I'd probably feel like it wasn't enough, but I think that's something I have to learn as well, getting out there and just doing it even if things aren't one hundred percent perfect. I have to learn to improvise. I have to learn to make decisions in the moment and to remember things, but at the same time, hold my own when things don't go right. I think that it will come at the exact time that it's meant to, and I think I'm going to surprise a lot of people and exceed a lot of expectations and have a smile on my face the whole time. If I don't, I'm probably suppressing it. This is the most fun I've ever had in my entire life, without a doubt. I don't often wake up in the morning this sore and this happy. I used to wake up sore and think, 'I'm tired forever now. I'm done forever.

I'm just going to sit until 2030.' There were days where it felt like I was going to be tired forever. I had no motivation to do anything. But ever since I started doing this, I'm more motivated every day. I'm genuinely excited about everything I have to do for the day. I want to do it so badly that no ache or pain on my body is going to hold me back."

CHAPTER 26
We Don't Set the Bar, We Are The Bar

MARCH 12, 2018: *MONDAY NIGHT RAW*

Braun Strowman wins the tag team battle royal by himself, defeating The Miztourage, Titus Worldwide, The Good Brothers, The Revival, and the team of Heath Slater and Rhyno, earning his shot at The Bar and their *Raw* tag team titles come *WrestleMania*. But who will be Braun's partner? "We will probably find out when his partner walks out during *WrestleMania*," says Cesaro, one-half of the tag team champions. "They like to keep us in the dark. Everyone thinks we know things months in advance, but when Braun won the battle royal, we found out like everyone else, on *Raw*, that day."

"I don't think Braun Strowman even knows who his partner is going to be," adds Sheamus, The Bar's other half who is looking forward to his moment in New Orleans. "I think it's something that the WWE Universe hasn't seen before, and it's going to be fun. That's what *WrestleMania* is all about: excitement, spectacle, and fun. That's what The Bar is all about. We're both living our dreams. We were both kids who watched WWE and dreamed of being in *WrestleMania*, and now we're going in as

the champions, and that's a pretty cool thing to say, a pretty cool dream to live."

The funny thing is, before The Bar was ever put together, Cesaro had told Sheamus that he was done with tag team wrestling. "When League of Nations was started, I told him, 'I don't want to be with anybody.' I was coming off the team with Tyson Kidd, which was an awesome tag team that got cut short because of Tyson's injury, so I didn't want to team with anybody else," says Cesaro. But everything changed after Cesaro and Sheamus were put together as opponents in a Best of Seven series by *Raw*'s then–General Manager Mick Foley. "We always clicked as opponents," explains Cesaro. "We both have a chip on our shoulders because we were both picked in the last round of the *Raw* and *SmackDown* draft. Then we got put in the Best of Seven and the first match was at the *SummerSlam* pre-show, so that just added to that chip on our shoulders. But we got to travel the world with the Best of Seven, with one of the matches being non-televised in London, and they showed clips of it on *Raw*, which hasn't been done in a long, long time. So that was cool. Then we were put together by Mick Foley, and we were both like, 'What the hell?' But we were both determined to make it as good as possible. We're both very competitive individuals, and we push each other inside and outside of the ring. But to be honest, probably neither of us thought it was going to be as successful as it has been. And we haven't even really started yet, we're still going strong."

"It has been a crazy journey," adds Sheamus. "When we were first put together, we didn't know where we were going to go, and now just over a year later, we're four-time tag team champs, and we're headed to *WrestleMania* as the *Raw* tag team champs for the second year in a row. We've outlasted everybody. Nobody thought we could beat The New Day. We beat The New Day. Nobody thought we could outlast the Hardys, we outlasted the Hardys. The Shield got back together and it was a great reunion, everybody thought it was fantastic, and we outlasted them. Now we're going against Strowman. Same thing. We're definitely one of the most underappreciated and underrated teams in

WWE. Every time we go out there, we steal the show, we have the best match, and we continue to carry the tag team straps on our shoulders. We're the best at what we do, and there's no stopping us. At the same time I still feel like people don't give us the credit we deserve. I've actually felt that way for a lot of my career. I feel like I constantly need to prove to people why I'm the best, but that's what happens when you are the best. There are people who are put on a higher pedestal than we are, even though we are way better when we go out there and perform."

Both men describe their relationship as being more like brothers than simply tag team partners, with Cesaro saying, "We talk all the time. We talk and text all day long. We give each other crap like brothers, we treat each other like brothers, we get into fights like brothers, and we're extremely close. We were acquaintances before, and now we're best friends."

The on-screen chemistry is undeniable, and in just over a year, The Bar has become one of the most successful and dominant tag teams of the past decade. "I think even if we ever go off and go after singles titles, we'll never break up," says Sheamus. "We started off as singles Superstars, and we can step in and out of The Bar whenever we want. I think it would be great if we could have singles titles along with the tag team titles. The amazing thing about our run together is that everything has been organic. Just look at our entrance, for example. Our entrance wasn't overproduced. It wasn't put together in a WWE studio, it wasn't focus-tested. Each thing that was put into our entrance was organic. We did something, we liked it, and we did it again. When I came back as a heel, we wanted to spotlight my pale skin, so we had the lights drop, then when the lights came back on, it was blinding and my pale skin would be shown as an effect. Combine that with Cesaro, and our back-to-back thing happened organically. Then we chopped the music together and went from there. In our early days, we wore our own getup, but then we started merging our gear. We wanted to wear jackets with kilts. I brought the kilts in, he brought the suit

jackets, and now we have more of army jackets. We're evolving all the time. Everything has been organic — our entrance, our partnership, our gear — and I think that's why it has been so special."

"New Day showed tag teams can be cool, and if you're on a great team, it can be so much more fun because you can play off each other," adds Cesaro. "Next thing you know, the Hardys came back, The Shield came back, The Usos were on fire, and all of a sudden you had all of these great teams competing and trying to one-up each other. Then we started bringing tag team wrestling to new levels. We main-evented pay-per views, we main-evented live events, we main-evented *Raw*. All of the top acts were in the ring with us, and we always delivered. We don't just set the bar, we are the bar. It's not just a saying — it's what we believe."

The Bar not only delivered amazing matches, but they acciden-tally delivered one of the most iconic injuries in recent WWE history, leading to Cesaro's bloody mouth and missing teeth going viral across social media. "I hit the metal turnbuckle pole with my teeth, and my

teeth were knocked up into my gums," explains Cesaro. "It was bleeding a lot and the doctor looked at it and thought they were gone, but they weren't knocked out, just up. It was a big match for us — it was for the tag team titles — and it's just part of what me and Sheamus do every night. We don't just play the part of Superstar, we breathe it, we eat it, we sleep it, and there was never a doubt in my mind that I could keep wrestling. It's funny because the next day, it was all over social media. It's good to know everybody got a good laugh at my expense. I feel like in situations like that, something bad happens, but I'm able to laugh about it. That's how I deal with bad stuff, I just make fun of it."

"I looked over and saw blood, and I was like, 'Where the hell is that blood coming from?'" laughs Sheamus. "Then I saw him and was like, 'Holy shit!' The doctor wanted us to end the match early, but we didn't. Cesaro is one tough son of a bitch, and he kept going. He kept pushing forward. We're fighters, and we've earned everything we've achieved. We're not just going to wuss out and not finish the match. It's not in our character. It's not who we are."

As for their match against Braun and his mystery partner, Cesaro says he is ready to roll with whoever shows up, even if he doesn't know who it will be beforehand. "There is a lot of stuff going on at all times within WWE, and in my time here, I've learned that anything can change, even after you've walked through the curtain," he explains. "Before, during, after the match, stuff is happening all the time, and plans change constantly. I like to be as prepared as I can walking out, but I don't read a textbook on what to do or imagine what could happen without knowing all of the facts. I wait until I know as much as possible, all the key facts and details, then I go from there in terms of planning out the match. And if that's not the case when I walk out, I'm perfectly fine just walking out to the ring and playing it out from there.

"Besides, I did the Big Swing on The Great Khali, I did the Big Swing on Tensai, and I'm pretty confident that if I wanted to, I can do the Big Swing on Braun Strowman."

CHAPTER 27
Fight for Your Dreams

MARCH 20, 2018: *SMACKDOWN LIVE*

Eight hours before *SmackDown LIVE* went to air from Dallas, WWE sent a Tweet that shook the Universe to its core.

> BREAKING: @WWEDanielBryan has been medically cleared to return to in-ring action!

"I genuinely got chills," says *205 Live* Superstar Cedric Alexander. "When I saw it on Twitter, I was like, 'Is this real? Is this a joke? Is today April Fool's Day?' I didn't know what was going on. Then I saw him in the locker room and he was getting ready to go out and make his comeback announcement, and I was like, 'Okay, don't mess with me, is this for real?' Even in the moment right before he told me, I didn't believe it."

But it was real, and it was glorious. "He's a tough little bastard," adds Randy Orton, who also couldn't wait to get to the arena and ask Bryan if the news was true. "He really works his ass off, so it's a really

good feeling to sec him come back. He had his dream taken away, and now he has a second chance."

"If you have this dream, and you keep fighting for it, it may come true, it might not," says Bryan, moments before walking out and delivering one of the most emotional speeches in WWE history. "It's never the end game. It's not the destination, it's the journey."

Bryan couldn't hide his smile as he led a deafening chorus of "Yes!" chants before finally addressing the crowd with the news they've been waiting years to hear. "A little over two years ago, when I was forced to retire, it was one of the hardest days of my life," says Bryan. "But I focused on one thing: on being grateful. And I kept on focusing on trying to be grateful. There were times when I was depressed about not being able to do what I love to do, but I focused on being grateful. And there were times when I was angry and I was mad that I couldn't do what I love to do, and I focused on being grateful. And I have a lot to be grateful for. I have an amazing family, I have amazing friends, I have the best fans in the world, and I also have an amazing, beautiful wife. And when I was depressed, when I was angry, and when I was trying to be grateful, she saw that all I wanted to do was get back in the ring, and she came to me and said, 'It's wonderful that you're grateful, but you need to fight, and you need to fight for your dreams.'

"She's the one who encouraged me to start to see specialists. So I went and I saw specialists, and then when the specialist gave me good reviews, she said, 'Go see another specialist.' And then she said, 'Go see another specialist.'

"And when I saw another specialist and they cleared me, she said, 'Listen, you need to fight for your dreams. That's what Daniel Bryan does. He fights for his dreams!' So then when I got depressed, I wasn't just grateful, I decided to fight. When I got angry about not being able to be in this ring, I wasn't just grateful, I decided to fight. There was a time when I wanted to quit, and instead of walking out, she got in my ear and said, 'You don't walk out, you fight, because you need to fight for your dreams. Fight for your dreams! Fight for your dreams! And if you fight for your dreams, your dreams will fight for you, because every hard thing seems impossible until it becomes real.'

"And over the last two months, I've asked WWE to relook at my case, and they sent me to the best neurologists all over the country. And all of these neurologists, every specialist, every doctor I've seen has said the same thing and that is this: You are cleared. There was a time when being cleared to compete in the WWE ring seemed impossible, but now it is real."

The news sent shockwaves not only backstage but through the creative plans for *WrestleMania 34*. What once looked like Shane McMahon and a mystery partner (possibly Dolph Ziggler or even Vince McMahon) taking on Kevin Owens and Sami Zayn had been transformed into Daniel Bryan and Shane McMahon versus Owens and Zayn in a match that instantly became one of the most-anticipated bouts on the entire card, especially after Zayn and Owens viciously attacked Bryan to end the show, putting his newfound clearance to the test, complete with a KO apron powerbomb.

"Honestly, the gravity of his announcement and comeback didn't really hit me until the night we beat him up and the night he made the announcement that he was cleared," says Zayn. "I had been talking to Bryan and I knew he was trying to get cleared. I knew his brain had been good for some time; he was just seeing different neurologists and receiving different treatments, like oxygen chamber therapy and all this stuff. I've been keeping tabs on him for a while, and he's been feeling great, but he was also on this quest to get cleared. And the way the storyline was shaping up with Shane, it seemed like the only logical answer: if Shane was going to have any tag team partner, it was going to be Daniel Bryan. But Daniel Bryan had no idea when or if he'd ever get cleared, and then everything changed. That night, we went out to the ring, and Kevin and I beat him down, and the response was overwhelming. It was old-school heat. It wasn't like, oh, they're the bad guys, let's all play along. The WWE Universe was genuinely furious with us, and that's really cool in this day and age. Any time you get

an opportunity to pull out that real, intense anger from the audience, it's really special. My whole career, I've been a good guy, so I've never really felt that kind of heat, that level of anger that we felt when we went out there with Daniel Bryan that night.

"Him being cleared really came out of left field, but I'm thrilled for him because he's a friend and he's just an incredible talent. I personally believe he's the best of our generation and the best in a very, very long time. I think it's a huge asset to have him back, whether it's a one-night thing, whether he becomes a full-time member of the roster, or even a part-time member of the roster from here on out. It's an honor and a privilege to be a part of it, specifically in New Orleans, where during *WrestleMania XXX* he had his greatest moment of his career. I was there that night, waiting for him to come backstage when he won his title, so to be in the same building a few years later and to be in the same match with him is kind of crazy. It's exciting for me, both personally and professionally."

The night of the comeback, Zayn said that they weren't given any

guidelines on what moves could or could not be performed on Bryan, so Zayn went out and treated him like any other Superstar on the roster. "I got the vibe, definitely from the office and the powers that be, that they were nervous, and rightfully so," Zayn says. "But at the same time, it would be disrespectful to Daniel Bryan to treat him like he's made of glass or to treat him with kid gloves. He's a tough guy, and if he's been cleared by all of these specialists, then he's cleared. He's not damaged goods, he's not washed up, he's good to go, so as far as I'm concerned, I'm going to treat him just like I would any other Superstar. Obviously, I'm not going out of my way to injure anybody. I'm a professional and I take a lot of pride in not causing any serious damage. I'm not going to treat him like he's lesser talent. He doesn't need to be handled like a baby. That would be a sign of disrespect in my eyes, anyway — but maybe I'm warped."

Unfortunately for the match, the injury news didn't end with Bryan, as just a few weeks later, WWE announced that Shane McMahon was in the hospital dealing with diverticulitis and a hernia that needed surgery. McMahon elected to have his surgery after *WrestleMania*, and Zayn wasn't surprised by Shane-O-Mac's decision. "It's all crazy," laughs Zayn. "And what people don't know is my shoulders aren't great, and Kevin's back isn't so good right now. Now Shane has a hernia and diverticulitis, but we're all pros and we're all committed. It has been a great storyline and it has been eight months in the making if you go back to *Hell in a Cell*. So in that regard, of all of these *WrestleMania* matches, this is the one storyline that has the most time invested. Hernia be damned, shoulder be damned, back be damned, concussions be damned . . . we're going to make the most of this opportunity. We're going to give this storyline what it deserves."

The storyline jump-started Zayn's first-ever heel turn. "It has been different," admits Zayn. "And Kevin would have a bit of a different perspective on it than I do. Full disclosure: he was more apprehensive about it than I was when it first happened. And understandably so, because he was in a better position than I was in. I was really just spinning my wheels right before I pulled him off the table at *Hell in a Cell*. All of a sudden, I'm thrust into a top storyline with Shane McMahon, the Commissioner of *SmackDown*. It was great; I was able to have a character rejuvenation while at the same time, I was able to be a part of something that mattered. When I say I was spinning my wheels, I felt like I had a lot to contribute and was not in a position to contribute. Now all of a sudden, I'm in a position to be an important part of the show, and the longer I'm with this company the more I realize that any time you get those windows, you can't take them for granted because they really are fleeting. These moments come and go, and there are ebbs and flows for everybody. Look at John Cena. Sometimes he's the world champion and he's the main act, and sometimes he takes more of a backseat. I'm not John Cena, so I don't know how he reacts to it, but certainly for me, going from a situation where I wasn't contributing to a storyline where I'm able to really add something to the show is something I'm adjusting to, but it definitely feels good to be in the position I'm in right now. And that's just from a personal standpoint. For fifteen-plus years, I've been a good guy, now all of a sudden I'm getting to explore all of these new things, which is good. It gives you more of a broader range, and if you look ahead, I think it will make me an even better good guy one day. When the WWE Universe sees the full three hundred sixty degrees of that range — the good, the bad, and the ugly — they like you even more and have an even deeper connection with your character.

"It's really a work in progress, and I'm still trying to figure it out. There are a lot of fine lines you need to walk. You want to be entertaining, but at the same time, you want to be believable. You want to be able to kick somebody's ass, but you need to be able to back off a little bit at the same time. It's a real fine balancing act. Right now, it's just about trying to find out that balance."

One of the first things heel Sami needed to figure out was how to successfully yank Owens off the table during the wicked Hell in a Cell Match — a match where Shane took flight off the top of the

cage, and it was up to Zayn to avoid disaster. "It was a miserable day for me," says Zayn. "All day I had a giant knot in my stomach due to the pressure of trying to pull off this Hollywood-level stunt that came down to milliseconds. I couldn't really rehearse, I kind of just had to do it, and I got only one take. I practiced pulling Kevin off the table earlier in the day, and he'd slip or our hands would come apart. He had lower back issues at the time, and if I didn't grab him hard enough, he legitimately couldn't sit up on his own quick enough to get off the table. He needed me to pull him off the table. I was trying to judge the timing, so I watched the footage of Shane jumping off the cage against Undertaker, and I was trying to time how long he was in the air. It seemed like I had 1.8 seconds to pull Kevin off the table. That's nothing! It was very, very stressful, and it came down to inches if you watch the footage back. It was so close to Shane McMahon crushing Kevin's head. I felt like I had their lives in my hands, and that was a very stressful thing for me. I had only one thing to do, but it was one extremely important thing. I'm just glad everybody lived to tell about it. It's one of those things that when you watch, you're like, 'Wow, crazy,' but you don't really realize the margin for error, and this is a life-defining error that could go down."

And while there's no cage dive to prepare for in New Orleans, Zayn still expects everyone in the match, but especially Bryan, to go all-out. "It's not just because this is his comeback — that's just the kind of performer he has always been," says Zayn. "I don't think I can rate anybody higher as a performer than I rate Daniel Bryan. I have infinite respect for him as a performer and as a person. To expect anything less than one hundred percent from him would be foolish. I expect to get the best from Daniel Bryan, I expect to get the best of Shane McMahon no matter what his health is, because he has that tunnel vision, he has that commitment. You need to have a missing screw in your head if you really want to make it in this business, and everybody in this match is missing that screw."

CHAPTER 28

Setting the Stage

MARCH 26, 2018: MERCEDES-BENZ SUPERDOME

During *WrestleMania* week, more than 1,000 people will work inside the Mercedes-Benz Superdome to build the stage, light the lights, and capture everything inside the stadium for the millions watching world-wide. Two weeks before the big show even starts, hundreds of workers have already descended on New Orleans to start creating the visuals that will set the tone and feel for the most important WWE event of the year. One of the men most intimately involved in helping shape those images is Live Director of Television Marty Miller, a 24-year WWE employee who has elevated his career from cameraman (he was once knocked into the Hell in a Cell cage by a flying R-Truth) to the man in charge of making all of those camera cuts the WWE Universe likes to debate after every show. "This year's set is being designed by Jason Robinson, who designs all of our sets and is one of the most creative people not only in WWE but in the whole entertainment industry," says Miller. "I freelanced for years doing major events like the Super Bowl and the World Series, and Jason is probably the most creative person I've met. We're really blessed to have a person like him. My job is to display that set in the best light not only to the live audience but to the television audience at home. From a television perspective, as a director, I collaboratively work with my team, which are the camera guys, and we try to capture the vision of Kevin Dunn and Jason and transfer that to the screen through whatever cameras we're using and the way we shoot it. That's pretty much our goal from the television side. It's tough because we want to do Jason's and Kevin's work justice so that their vision is felt through the television screen. It's my responsibility that the person who is watching from home on an iPhone or an iPad or a big-screen TV can also feel that stage and see that stage like a live fan does."

And while the set takes up to two weeks to fully build, there are a variety of steps that need to be taken into consideration. Luckily, having worked the Superdome already, for *WrestleMania XXX*, the team has a head start and already understands the intricacies of the stadium itself. While the set is under construction, WWE also sends a group to handle all of the cabling and wiring for television. "Once the set is built, we can then go in and start building TV around it," Miller explains. "In the weeks leading up to *WrestleMania*, we have meetings about what types of hardware we're going to use — whether we're using Skycam or rail cam or Steadicams — how we're going to implement these into our production, and how we can make things both different and good. We meet with the pyro guys to make sure we don't miss any pyro cues. We work with Jason and his lighting guys to make sure we capture all of the entrances just right. We try to determine how we can best utilize the hardware we have. We really take a lot of time in developing the look of each *WrestleMania* and how we go about capturing that look. Once the actual *WrestleMania* week comes, we do a lot of rehearsing and dialing in on all of the stuff that we normally don't have, such as the Skycam or a helicopter or the extra Steadicams, and we get all of the guys up to speed on how we do television. Again, things can change at any second, so if someone sees something they don't like, we can change it. We can change it up to the last minute. And during *WrestleMania* week, there's no normal concept of time. There's before *WrestleMania*, there's *WrestleMania*, and that's it. There's no Wednesday, Thursday, Friday, Saturday, Sunday . . . to us, it's like just one big day once we're down there. You're constantly working. You're getting sleep where you can, but you make the best of it. You know it's going to be nonstop, twenty-hour days, but you attack it, and to our crew's credit, that's what we do. It's a grind that week, but we all enjoy it. We all go through our ups and downs, and I'm not going to say there aren't arguments — there are always some disagreements — but at the end of the day, everyone agrees that we need to put the best product on television. The *WrestleMania* day itself, we get started early on Saturday, and we're there until the wee hours of the morning, but then we're right back there at 8 a.m. on Sunday to start rehearsals again. We go through rehearsals until three or four o'clock, then we have meetings with the agents and producers to determine what's going on in these matches, so we don't miss anything during the actual show. We need to make sure everyone is on the same page. Then *WrestleMania* starts, and that's actually the best feeling, because this is the moment everybody has been waiting for. There's no looking back now, so you go full force until the end. You just hope you're prepared and you're ready for that moment. For the most part, from a cameraman's perspective, your adrenaline level is higher and you're much more focused at *WrestleMania* than a normal *Monday Night Raw*. You have to be, since there is anywhere from sixty thousand people to a hundred thousand people at the live event, and you can't help but feel that energy, whether you're in the arena or in the truck. From a TV standpoint, it's all about trying to capture that feeling that the talent is trying to convey to the audience as perfectly as possible, striking the right balance for both the television and live audience."

And for Miller, he admits the crew feels the added pressure of working *WrestleMania*, but it's more about making sure that the talent is represented in the best way possible than thoughts of messing up

on a single-camera cut or shot. "When I look at *WrestleMania*, it's the culmination of a year of hard work for the Superstars, and that's where the pressure comes in," says Miller. "You want to do them justice on their day. The Superstars train so hard and for so long, and they dream of walking through that curtain of *WrestleMania* on the biggest day of their professional lives, in an arena with up to a hundred thousand people and an elaborate set and stage, and I want to be able to capture all of that excitement and emotion in a way that they're proud of. I want to make sure that we match their expectations. It's not about making mistakes, it's about fulfilling the expectations of not only the Superstars but of the WWE Universe too. We want to make sure they're extraordinarily satisfied. As the director, you have to make sure the Superstars and the WWE Universe love what they see when they watch it back."

As for the hotly debated camera cuts, Miller responds, "Yeah, that's me. Basically, Kevin Dunn and the producers run the traffic and run the show from A to Z. I'm more of the meat-and-potatoes guy. I fill in all of the live content you see. Kevin is more involved with branding and talking to the announcers and making sure the right replay gets on the air. I'm more concerned with telling the stories through the cameras, but obviously we're working hand in hand. We're working as a team to execute that, so I'm following his lead. I need to be on the same page he is, so that when I come in, I'm on the right shot to tell the story.

"From a live perspective, you can always go back and go, 'Ooh, I wish I would've stayed on that shot a little longer,' or 'I should've cut off of that sooner,' but for the most part, you have to feel it in the moment. At the same time, you have to tell the story, so sometimes you need to cut away from one angle to the second angle in order to get the other person's reaction, because you know that reaction is only going to be there for a split second. It's not like a movie where you can shoot it five different ways and then you have the opportunity to go back and edit it. This is live, so you want to find that right balance between capturing the shot you have and telling the story. It is really instinctive; it takes some time to learn that. Some nights, just like an athlete, you feel like you're in a groove and you can't miss. Other nights you feel like you're a split second off on everything, but that's just the way live television goes. During *WrestleMania*, obviously, you want to have one of those nights where everything goes your way. You live on the edge with live television. Anything can and will happen, you just have to feel your way through it. I will tell you as a cameraman, director — I've worked on basketball, hockey, football, entertainment — there is nothing more challenging than working a WWE live event and putting it on television. It's the most difficult show in the world to do, without a doubt."

CHAPTER 29
Outta Nowhere

MARCH 27, 2018: *SMACKDOWN LIVE*

Rusev earns his way into the Fatal 4-Way for the United States Championship at *WrestleMania* thanks to his victory, alongside Jinder Mahal, over the team of Bobby Roode and United States Champion Randy Orton. But at what price? Rusev's Machka Kick to Orton's jaw ends the match, but it was a kick that looked so fierce everyone from backstage personnel to Orton's own father, WWE Hall of Famer "Cowboy" Bob Orton, thought Randy was injured.

"It looked like he kicked my face off," laughs Orton. "My dad actually called me and was like, 'Son, are you okay?' Rusev's kicks look stiff enough that my old man actually called me. I walked back through the curtain after the match and everybody was like, 'Are you okay?' He never even touched me. When you have everyone in Gorilla biting, that means the WWE Universe is biting, that means you're doing your job."

Orton, whose *WrestleMania* legacy kicked off in *WrestleMania XX* inside Madison Square Garden, sees his family's legacy and ties to WWE history as just one reason why he's looking forward to his title defense in New Orleans. "My dad appearing in the first *WrestleMania* definitely helps make it mean more to me," says Orton. "It already means so much, but having that personal connection is pretty cool. The first *WrestleMania* was inside Madison Square Garden, and then twenty years later, I debuted at *WrestleMania XX* at Madison Square Garden, and my father was there for that match; it was such a great moment. It was a high-profile match, me and Batista against Mick Foley and The Rock, and I ended up winning the match. *WrestleMania* in itself is important to everybody, especially everyone in the locker room. But to me, it's just a little extra special of an occasion."

And to Orton, his *WrestleMania 34* match is special because of the three men he'll be sharing the ring with, three men Orton holds in great respect. "When you look at Bobby Roode, I would compare him to Triple H," says Orton. "He's a real special talent. When we go out there and the bell rings, I can put a headlock on Bobby, and I can work that headlock for a minute, even though the WWE Universe isn't exactly screaming or yelling, because there's not much going on, we are just getting started telling our story. Bobby will take that headlock and he'll sell it for the rest of the match. He makes that headlock worth something. He's really good at selling. That's something I was always really good at. Sometimes you're in the ring with a guy who just wants to go-go-go-go-go, but it's not about how many bumps you take or how much offense you get in. Bobby wants to work with you. There's a fine line between being stiff in a dangerous way and being stiff in a safe way, and Bobby is stiff in a safe way. His moves look good, he sells good, he busts his ass, he's got the look, and he doesn't try to do hundreds of moves, he sticks to what he's good at. He's a perfect opponent for me because I enjoy the storytelling aspect. How Bobby sells his neck after taking a neck-breaker early on in the match really just adds so much to the story we're trying to tell.

"Rusev is another guy who is great, and I'm not just here to put everybody over, because I don't think everybody is good, that's for damn sure. Rusev is another one, like Bobby, who loves what he's

doing. He doesn't rush, so he knows when to settle down and when is the right time to get physical. I'm really happy Rusev is in this match. I trust him and I know he is going to be there when I need him to be there. He's got the look, he's got the moves, and he has all the little things that help make a perfect WWE Superstar."

The third opponent, Jinder Mahal, has been working with Orton both in front of the camera and behind the scenes since their 2017 rivalry over the WWE Championship, and Orton sees big things in Mahal's future thanks to the Superstar's work ethic and intangibles. "Jinder holds a special place in my heart," explains Orton. "About a year ago, when I won the championship against Bray Wyatt at *WrestleMania* in the iconic bug match, and Vince pulled me aside and he told me he wanted me to work with Jinder. There were a lot of meetings about the WWE Network expanding into India and the WWE wanting a bigger presence in India, so Vince wanted to take Jinder, this Indian WWE Superstar, and see if he could use that, business-wise, to get more people into the product. So Vince pulled me aside about twenty-five

days after I won the championship and asked me what I thought of losing the title to Jinder, and I thought it was a great idea.

"I'm at a point in my career where I don't need the title. Don't get me wrong, I love having the title, but I didn't think losing the title was going to hurt me. And Jinder really stepped up not only in the ring but how he carries himself backstage. You won't catch me in a suit, but he dressed the part as champion. Jinder went above and beyond: he got the Rolex, he was coming to the arena in these suits, and it sounds silly, but he played the role of WWE Champion. Not only that, but he's a great guy, he's great in the locker room, and he busts his ass. He's as hungry or even hungrier than anyone else in that locker room. So it was great for me to help him in his craft and to tell those stories in the ring. I still help him from time to time, but it's less and less as he's really catching on. He's becoming a top guy, not only because of the look but because he's honing his craft to become a more well-rounded WWE Superstar. When I was younger, Ric Flair and Triple H took me under their wing — that's how I came up — so I wanted to pass along some knowledge to Jinder in that same way. You can help out with your knowledge and, chances are, you come out better for it too."

And while Orton relishes the opportunity to pass down knowledge, the Legend Killer said he still has plenty of years left in his career. "I'm only thirty-eight, so while I'm no spring chicken . . . I started so early, and I've been around for such a long time — people think I'm older than I really am," laughs Orton. "It's funny because some of those old-timers like Ric Flair still call me kid. I like that. When you look at my career, I was supposed to be a part of *WrestleMania XIX*, but I was injured, then a year later I was in the ring with The Rock. There's a lot of ups and downs, and it takes time to make it on the *WrestleMania* card. There are so many guys and girls who want to be in that battle royal just to get that experience of being at *WrestleMania*. I think this is going to be the thirteenth *WrestleMania* I've performed in, and every year, it seems like the roster gets more and more crowded and it's tougher for you to get on the card. It's really a right-place, right-time kind of thing, and if you don't find yourself on the card or in a spot that you like, then work even harder the next year and hopefully you can move up."

Orton's chance this year opened up when he won the United States Championship at *Fastlane*, defeating Bobby Roode in an old-school mat classic that would eventually lead to the Fatal 4-Way at *Mania*. "The way it happened, I wasn't planning on winning this championship," says Orton. "I won the IC Championship in 2003 against Rob Van Dam, and I had it for six or seven months, then I went on to the World Championship and I just never looked back. Being a Grand Slam Champion wasn't ever one of my goals, but when you look back and you have *Royal Rumble* victories and you've won multiple World Championships, and you've main-evented *WrestleMania*, then all of a sudden somebody tells you that if you win this match against Bobby Roode, you'll be one of about ten people in the history of the company who have become a Grand Slam Champion, it's really cool. It gives me the chance to show people that I still got it. The United States Championship, the IC Championship, those are the championships for guys who are usually in the mid-card but have the potential to one day be the top guy. It's a stepping stone, for lack of a better term, and now, like Jinder, I can help work with a lot of these other guys and hopefully give them some knowledge on how to make it to that next level."

In the meantime, Orton will continue to shine not only in the WWE ring but on social media thanks to the "RKO Outta Nowhere" videos that have accumulated millions of views online — videos where users insert Orton RKOing random people and celebrities as they come crashing down on everything from pavement to snow to the soccer pitch. "When it first happened, I thought it was funny, but a lot of that stuff is a flash in the pan, and a week goes by, and everybody has moved on," says Orton. "That's how ninety-nine percent of things that go viral seem to work. But it has been three or four years now, and there's still an uptick in the amount of views and likes, and people are still making new videos. They're inserting me in *Star Wars* trailers and *Jurassic Park* trailers and Marvel trailers, and now I'm RKOing a dinosaur or Iron

Man. It's incredible how much time people spend inserting me into these videos. I wish I could shake the hand of the guy who started this, because there's no denying that this has helped me. People who don't watch WWE will see me and ask, 'Aren't you the RKO guy?' You know you have something special when people who aren't part of the WWE Universe know who you are and know your finishing move."

Will it be an RKO out of nowhere that gives Orton yet another memorable *Mania* moment? Orton is not only hoping to create that special highlight for *WrestleMania 34*, but he's already looking ahead and hoping for something even bigger at *WrestleMania 35*. "When I heard Daniel Bryan was coming back, I was excited because I know he's a guy I can go with," says Orton. "He's someone people really care about, and that's a hard thing to achieve. He's a good guy, he does the right thing, and people sympathize with him. AJ Styles and Daniel Bryan are the top two guys people care about right now, so when I heard he was coming back, I started to think about storylines we might be able to pull off together. I've had some of my favorite matches against Daniel Bryan, and I'd love to build up a great storyline that can lead into next year's big show."

CHAPTER 30
Stay Loud

APRIL 2, 2018: *MONDAY NIGHT RAW*

John Cena has been calling out Undertaker for weeks to no response. No Dead Man, no druids, no hellish gongs from his theme song. "Hey, Undertaker," Cena tells the *Raw* crowd, "it's obvious that you left your hat in the ring, but it's clear to everybody here that you left your balls at home." Savage. But with no response, John Cena is a man without a match, and he would head to New Orleans as a fan to watch the show from the seats. It's a storyline that has wrestling journalists debating online. Is Undertaker showing up? Didn't he just retire last year? If he is showing up, will there be a match? Or simply a confrontation that leads to a match at *WrestleMania 35*? It's the first time in WWE history that a match of this magnitude has been teased but not officially announced heading into *WrestleMania*. And according to everyone from Creative to members of the locker room, only a handful of people know the actual payoff.

"I think that with Kid Rock being inducted into the Hall of Fame and Kid Rock also singing 'The American Bad Ass' song that Taker used when he wasn't Undertaker, I think that Taker did retire last year, but he's going to come back this year as the American Bad Ass," guesses Randy Orton. "He's going to go out there for one last match and go out on a high note by beating John Cena. That's what I think will happen."

"I don't even want to know what's going to happen until it happens," says *WWE Raw* and *SmackDown LIVE* announcer Corey Graves, who will be calling all of the action come *WrestleMania 34*. "I like to know as little as possible. I feel like it actually helps me if I don't know what's going to happen. It's a lot easier to be surprised than to act surprised. Last year, for example, I had no idea that the Hardys were coming back. When their music hit, I had the same reaction as everybody else in that stadium. That was as genuine a reaction that you're going to get in anything, and I loved it. It was cool because I've been a fan of those guys forever, so to actually be fooled, that's still part of the fun for me. On any given broadcast, being surprised is what has made a wrestling fan out of me, and it has always been that way . . . not knowing what to expect. So I love being in the dark and just being able to react."

Even with Undertaker's potential return, the match Graves can't wait to see is the main event featuring WWE Universal Champion Brock Lesnar against number one contender Roman Reigns. "You have the highest level of fans from all over the globe coming to *WrestleMania*, the smart fans," says Graves. "And I'm sure they will be very vocal and have their opinions, but one thing that's indisputable when it comes to Roman Reigns and Brock Lesnar is when they get in the ring and they do what they do, it doesn't matter what you think is supposed to happen or what you think the company is trying to force you to feel, by the end of the match, everybody in the stadium is going to be on their feet and lost in a great match."

Leading into *Mania*, Lesnar and Reigns upped the ante on violent attacks, including Reigns being beat down while handcuffed and even taking a brutal-looking F5 chest-first on the steel steps. At the go-home show before New Orleans, Paul Heyman offered "not a prediction, it's a spoiler" that Lesnar would pin Reigns in the middle of the *WrestleMania 34*

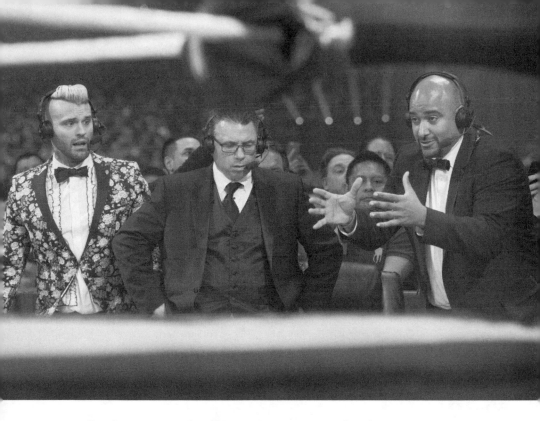

ring for the one-two-three. Five Superman punches later, Lesnar was down, but then again, The Beast is never out, springing to his feet to deliver the final F5 before *Mania*. Says Graves, "I'm sure after the main event is over and the winner is announced at *WrestleMania*, the WWE Universe will complain — because that's what fans of anything do these days, rather than just enjoy it for what it is — but in my opinion, Roman and Brock are going to tear it down in New Orleans."

Graves, who is headed to New Orleans after calling the final *SmackDown* before *Mania* on Tuesday night, says he's looking forward to the big show, even if he's not so fond of the memories New Orleans holds, as it's the site of the injury that forced the former NXT star out of the ring and into broadcasting. "It was at Axxess before *WrestleMania XXX*," remembers Graves. "So it's kind of weird now going back there — everything has come full circle. That injury sent me on a whole new career path, and now here I am four years later and I'm getting ready to call *WrestleMania* as one of the new voices of WWE. In a weird way, it's a little poetic, and I'm just excited to get to be a part of it."

Graves studied for and practiced his new career at the Performance Center and during *NXT* broadcasts before finally being called up to the "big leagues." Says Graves, "When it comes to my career, nothing went according to plan. Once I started this new career path, getting the chance to call *WrestleMania* was always the goal. You always want to be a part of *WrestleMania*, and there's no reason why I can't still be a part of it. My voice will live on for many *WrestleMania*s to come. It was always the goal, but it's something so ingrained in me. It's the life here, you don't have time to stop and think about the magnitude of what you're doing.

"Last year was my first *WrestleMania* and I remember calling the pre-show and not really thinking too much about it, but then when the actual show started and the jet flew over the stadium, that's when it hit me like, 'Wow, I'm calling *WrestleMania*.' This year is going to be a little different because I'm the only guy who calls both *Raw* and *SmackDown*, so I'm going to be the only one who calls all of *WrestleMania*. It's going to be a task in and of itself, but I got through the *Royal Rumble*, so I think I'll be able to hold up pretty well. I just want to make sure all of the stories get told. I'm pretty notorious for not doing too much prep work — I'm more reactionary — but I like to think that of all the work that I do, my calls during *WrestleMania* are the calls that will live forever. If I have a cool story in my back pocket, I'll have it ready for that day because I know how many people are watching the show. *WrestleMania* is the pinnacle to all of the talent, and I feel like I'd be doing the talent a disservice if I didn't treat the event with the respect it deserves. They work their whole lives and all year long to have that *WrestleMania* moment, so if I can provide the appropriate soundtrack to it and have some fun with it, that's where my focus is."

One thing Graves said that the WWE Universe might not realize, however, is that it can be tough for announcers to lock in to that focus — while they're calling the matches, they can hear the likes of Vince McMahon in their ear pieces, giving them direction. "We have a plethora of voices in our heads at all times," says Graves. "Between the producers and the boss himself, if he has something that he wants to get across or there's something he sees that we didn't see — sometimes you're in the middle of a thought and you're trying to formulate a sentence and someone's talking to you about something completely unrelated. It can be a bit confusing. There were a few times where I went back and watched a match over and I was like, 'Oh yes, he was talking to me at that point.' I'll know exactly where I want to go and he's telling me something completely different, related to something totally opposite, but it's his mindset at the time. It happens, but you get used to it. It's tough to have someone try to talk to you while you're trying to talk. That was the toughest thing for me as I trained to become a broadcaster. It took a lot of practice to be able to speak through it."

Besides having to listen and talk at the same time, Graves said the other biggest thing people don't realize is the sheer amount of information the announce team has to learn before every event. "The amount of information we have to process and turn around is pretty crazy," says Graves. "Not only are we the narrators of the story, the story is constantly evolving and changing from segment to segment, match to match. Things change on the fly all the time and we'll be getting information in our ears about what's going on and we need to make sense of it. It's information overload, and I know a lot of times people will say, 'hey, you never mentioned this' or 'you never even called out this move that they did,' but sometimes it's a thankless position where you want to make five things happen, but you only have time for two."

Add the chaos and unpredictability of a flying body or two headed his way, and Graves expects the unexpected when it comes to *WrestleMania*. "You always have to be on your toes," laughs Graves. "Every once in a while, we get a heads-up beforehand, but more often than not when we see people coming, we know it's time to get up and get out of the way. Sometimes guys will switch directions and come flying over the announce table. On *SmackDown*, someone gets launched over the table every couple of weeks, and if you're not ready to react, you're going to be on the wrong end of Randy Orton one of these days. Same holds true for *WrestleMania*. We're going to be right down there by the action, so you never know what's going to happen or who might come flying your way."

CHAPTER 31
The Superfan

APRIL 4, 2018: BOURBON STREET

Lifelong WWE fan Jose Sanchez has just arrived in New Orleans and is walking down Bourbon Street when he spots a familiar face ahead of him. "It was Xavier Woods," says 37-year-old Sanchez. "He was just out walking the street and saying hi to fans. I was like, 'You're braving the streets early. You have a busy weekend.' To Sanchez, getting the chance to talk to Woods is just the start of his *WrestleMania* vacation. New Orleans marks Sanchez's 12th time to *Mania*, and while he says he was overwhelmed by the size and scope of the Dallas event back in 2016, he much prefers the more intimate nature of New Orleans and Bourbon Street. "*WrestleMania* week is such a fan-crazed event, that WWE just takes over the city. *WrestleMania 32* in Dallas was such a spectacle, the show itself was bananas, but Dallas is such a big city, and all of the events were so spread out, you didn't have the same vibe as you get in New Orleans where everything happens in a much more condensed area. That's why you see some of the boys just walking down the street and hanging out. Matt Hardy was out walking the street in his Woken character, Elias did an open mic night . . . there is always something happening that you don't want to miss."

And sometimes, the can't-miss moments are as simple as seeing another wrestling fan walk by with a familiar shirt. "Any time someone walks by in a Rusev Day shirt, it was like everyone on Bourbon Street starts chanting," says Sanchez. "For a week, I couldn't get Aiden English out of my head. It's crazy how WWE fans bond over a T-shirt or some dude cosplaying as the Macho Man. At one point, we walked by this guy dressed like Darth Vader who was blaring Kurt Angle's music. Everyone who walked by would join in, 'You suck, you suck!' He was digging it."

Sanchez, who works as a freelance host and video-game content creator, cashed in his frequent flyer miles to fly from San Francisco to New Orleans for only $12, while a friend used hotel points so the two could share a room for free. "My flight had a layover in Las Vegas," says Sanchez, "and when I looked up, I saw a slot machine called Lobstermania. I figured, I'm going to *WrestleMania*, there's a slot machine called Lobstermania, this has to be a sign." Sure enough, Sanchez played the machine and won $200. "It has helped pay for my meals," Sanchez laughs. "Besides, we've learned to eat frugally. It's Willie's Chicken Shack just about every day."

And Sanchez isn't alone in his fandom (or frugality), as the WWE Universe floods the streets of New Orleans ready to chant and chow down. One of the most popular spots of the week is *WrestleMania* Axxess, with more than 25,000 fans attending from over 36 different countries and all 50 states. According to WWE officials, it's the interactive nature of Axxess that helps set it apart, as fans are able to get autographs and pictures with their favorite Superstars. Axxess also provides exhibits featuring memorabilia from the Evolution of Women's Wrestling — including items from Sensational Sherri, Alundra Blayze, Bull Nakano, Trish Stratus, Charlotte, and Asuka. Another exhibit features historical items from the 2018 WWE Hall of Fame class and an area dedicated to Hall of Famers who have been immortalized as bronze

statues, including Andre the Giant, Bruno Sammartino, Dusty Rhodes, Ric Flair, and Ultimate Warrior. In addition, multiple tournaments are held inside *WrestleMania* Axxess, each with major championship implications. Featured tourneys include the WWE United Kingdom Championship Invitational, NXT North American Invitational, NXT Tag Team Invitational, and NXT Women's Invitational. The tournaments begin on the Thursday and Friday sessions of Axxess and culminate on Sunday, with the winners of each tournament facing the respective champions from *NXT TakeOver: New Orleans*.

But that isn't all, as the nearly 300,000-square-foot exhibit also features a full-sized Elimination Chamber that enables fans to actually enter a pod to see first-hand what it's like inside the mammoth structure. An in-ring proposal that was set up with help from WWE staff in attendance turned out to be the biggest surprise of Axxess weekend, however. On the Saturday of *WrestleMania* weekend, the special fan's girlfriend was "selected" to participate in a contest inside the ring. She was blindfolded and told she had to touch each corner turnbuckle, but

when she reached the final corner, her boyfriend was there on one knee with the ring in hand. She said "yes" and the crowd erupted in cheers. From fans dressing as Undertaker and Sasha Banks to the ability to call historic matches as an announcer to real-life marriage proposals, Axxess is the hot spot for the WWE Universe in New Orleans.

"We worked alongside Mayor Mitch Landrieu and our local organizing committee partners for fourteen months to build a blueprint to again welcome the world to New Orleans," says John Saboor. "So many smiles on so many faces from so many fans throughout the globe."

"Last time I was in New Orleans, Daniel Bryan won the championship, but Bourbon Street was the saddest I had ever seen it because Undertaker lost," says Sanchez. "It was unbelievable how sad Bourbon Street was. That streak ending really stuck with people. But this year has a different vibe. The city has such a good energy about it for *WrestleMania*. There's a reason WWE keeps coming back, even if New Orleans is the place where streaks go to die.

"This is the biggest event of the year for me, and I make sure that if I go to only one wrestling event a year, it's the showcase. I can't wait to head to New York next year to see what kind of surprises WWE is going to pull off. Every year, it's something new, and it's almost become an addiction to try to get to these shows. I just need to book another layover in Las Vegas first to make sure I have enough money for the week." Lobstermania for the win.

CHAPTER 32
With My Baby Tonight

APRIL 6, 2018: HALL OF FAME

When it came to his guitar, "Double J" Jeff Jarrett was an equal-opportunity free swinger, smashing everyone from Gary Coleman to Chyna. The cocky heel eventually parted ways with WWE and, in his multiple stints in WCW, became a member of both the legendary Four Horsemen and nWo. But when Vince McMahon purchased WCW, he fired Jarrett live on TV in front of the world, with the words: "You know how Jeff spells his name, 'That's J-E-double-F,' well, you know what, I would suspect that it's spelled a different way after tonight, and that would be capital G–double O– double N–double E, gone."

"That was just good television," Jarrett says with a laugh, reflecting on the famous segment. That firing eventually led him to create his own wrestling federation, Total Nonstop Action, in hopes of building an alternative to the juggernaut that is WWE. The sequence of events led almost everybody in the industry to think that they'd never see Jarrett in WWE again. No *Royal Rumble* surprise appearance. No return to trade guitar shots with Elias. And definitely no Hall of Fame.

But in January, WWE shocked the wrestling community by announcing that Jarrett would be joining the likes of Goldberg, The Dudley Boyz, Mark Henry, Ivory, and Hillbilly Jim in the 2018 Hall of Fame. "I was shocked. It was a surreal moment," says Jarrett, about receiving the call from WWE officials. "It was a phone call in the morning in early January, and it was really a special phone call. Not really long in length, but it was straight to the point. They asked if I was interested, and there was a long pause and I let it sink in, but I was certainly honored and humbled for it to happen."

For Jarrett, he calls the entire journey an emotional experience. After getting the Hall of Fame call in early 2018, he's excited to continue to mend fences with Vince McMahon and company. Jarrett takes special pride in his Hall of Fame induction, as he sees it as an induction for his entire family, a family that has been in the wrestling business since his grandmother started promoting shows over 70 years ago. "I'm third generation in this business," says Jarrett. "My grandmother on one side of the family promoted and did a little bit of everything, except wrestle. I'm really accepting this on behalf of my entire family. I'm the lucky one who gets to be inducted. Out of all of the thousands, or even tens of thousands, who my family promoted or wrestled or watched, there are less than two hundred of us in the Hall of Fame. It's something where I'm very honored and humbled to be included. This class especially is really unique."

The unique class is headlined by Goldberg, whose shocking return to the WWE ring in 2016 led to both a run with the Universal Championship and an 86-second win over Brock Lesnar at *Survivor Series*. The former champ was inducted by Lesnar's advocate, Paul Heyman, after the two sports-entertainment icons grew close during the Goldberg/Lesnar rivalry and buildup to *WrestleMania 33*. "Surely, you must be wondering why the former owner of ECW is inducting the biggest star from WCW into the WWE Hall of Fame," laughs Heyman. "But it's a little difficult to find opponents for Brock Lesnar. We needed to find someone to kick Brock Lesnar's ass. We needed

to find someone to beat up Brock Lesnar and beat Brock Lesnar in such an authentic fashion that you would believe in it and buy into it. He's part of the greatest comeback in sports-entertainment history, and I couldn't be prouder than to be the one who inducts him on such a special night." A night of highlights that also included The Dudley Boyz putting a "production assistant" through a table, Ivory talking Gorgeous Ladies of Wrestling, and Mark Henry tearfully remembering the time his mom brought him to see Andre the Giant.

Before Henry and Heyman took the stage, however, it was Jarrett's turn to shine, as the man formerly known as Double J was inducted into the Hall of Fame by the Road Dogg, Brian James. "The Roadie" got his first shot in WWE as an assistant to Jarrett's Double J country music star persona, a character with a "hit" single, but it turned out it was James singing "With My Baby Tonight" all along. "It's like that song has taken on a life of its own," says Jarrett, laughing. "It was twenty-plus years ago when we did the song and the video, and that situation never really got a payoff, but here we are coming full circle, the ups and downs that Road Dogg and I have gone through together. It's really special for him. He's a second-generation wrestler. And it's really special for me to have him induct me. He is without a doubt the perfect choice, and I'm super honored that he's the one doing it." And the induction led to one of the most talked about moments of the night, as Jarrett and James performed "With My Baby Tonight" karaoke style while even getting some help from Double J fan Zack Ryder.

Reflecting back to when his country music persona started, Jarrett said that some things just write themselves. "For the first seven or eight years of my career, I was the good guy, I was the babyface. I was the guy from Music City, USA, with a unique name, a lot of double letters, two Js, two Fs, two Rs, two Ts. It just sort of rolled off the tongue. I've always been a big fan of country music — always have been, always will be. In the '90s, country music exploded with Garth Brooks and others, so it all just came together and fell into place. Vince is a visionary and a creative genius. I don't throw those words around lightly, but his track record speaks for itself. He has a knack for defining characters and he certainly did so with Double J."

As for his favorite WWE memories, Jarrett points out his time teaming with Owen Hart, as well as the run he had working with a crew of all-time greats. "When I look back at my time in WWE, I spent a lot of time in the ring with Scott Hall [Razor Ramon], Kevin Nash [Diesel], and Shawn Michaels. Those are special memories. My favorite partner was Owen Hart, we won the tag team gold, and he was just so much fun to be around. In terms of my favorite match, there was a series of matches, a two- or three-month run where it was me and Shawn versus Razor and Diesel, and we had the Roadie with us, so it was a lot of fun. The most charismatic guy out of all of us was the guy outside the ring, so it was really, really entertaining, hard-hitting, and fast action. We told a great story and it was an incredible roller-coaster ride. Singles matches are great, but when you have five guys like that together, it was something special every night."

In terms of current WWE product, Jarrett doesn't miss an episode. "The Miz is special," says Jarrett, explaining how important it is that Miz brought the storied tradition of the Intercontinental Championship back to the forefront. "You can't help but see the passion he has for his work, for his persona, and for his IC Championship. It comes across in his promos, in his work, and he believes with all his heart and soul in that Intercontinental Championship. There have been times where people held that championship but didn't put everything into it. He takes a lot of pride in that championship, and certainly I did, Shawn did, Razor did, and so did a lot of greats. I'm happy to see how he has revived the championship."

Jarrett is also keeping an eye on some former TNA talent that he helped introduce to a bigger audience years ago. "AJ Styles was in our very first match at TNA," says the new Hall of Famer. "He was the Grand Slam Champion, then we both left TNA at the same time and went to New Japan, and we were together in Japan. So I couldn't be happier for the guy. He's going into *WrestleMania* as the WWE Champion the same year I'm stepping onstage as one of the Hall of Fame inductees. AJ has got some years under his belt, but he has maintained his very, very high level of performance for years now. When it's all said and done — and he's far from being all said and done — he is going to go down as one of the greats, no doubt. Then you have Bobby Roode going after the United States Championship, a title I've held. Samoa Joe, the injuries have cost him, but all three guys are really, really special. Talent is what has gotten them to the top, and it has gotten them to the top of every promotion they've worked in, and their attitude keeps them there. I'm really happy for those guys."

But now that Jarrett's in the Hall of Fame, will we see him more regularly on WWE TV? Maybe even get that *Royal Rumble* appearance or showdown with Elias? "When I look at Elias, the dude can obviously sing, he can play, so it's not a gimmick — that is him," says Jarrett. "He's playing an extension of his personality. I have a lot of respect for

the guy, watching through my big screen, because he evokes emotion. He's obviously getting a role now and I'm excited to see him move up to the next level and see how things play out. The guy has a ton of talent. But for me, right now, my only contact with WWE has been about the Hall of Fame and press and Axxess. Never say never, but I'm not concerned with one more match or anything like that right now because I don't want to miss any moment, any step of the way. At the end of the day, *WrestleMania 34* is the first opportunity in my entire life to go to a wrestling show, the biggest show of the year, and have zero responsibility other than to put on a suit and wave to the crowd. I'm just as excited to go to *Mania* as I am to go to the Hall of Fame. It's going to be a very special weekend."

CHAPTER 33
The One and Only

APRIL 7, 2018: *NXT TAKEOVER*

When Vince McMahon asked Paul "Triple H" Levesque about running a live NXT event the weekend of *WrestleMania 31* in Santa Clara, Levesque was excited about the possibility but nervous at the same time. The proposed site for the event, the San Jose Events Center, holds a capacity of 5,000 people, and Levesque, who had recently been promoted to the Executive Vice President of Talent, Live Events, and Creative, was worried how many people would show up to watch his next generation of WWE talent. "The show ended up being one of the most buzzed-about things all weekend," says a proud Levesque. The event sold out almost immediately and was attended by everyone from Seth Rollins and Shawn Michaels to Kevin Nash, Scott Hall, Stephanie McMahon, and even Vince himself, as everyone wanted to see what Levesque's underground "third brand" was all about. "The energy inside the arena was insane," adds Levesque. "The event was such a massive success and it really helped lay the foundation for what was to come."

Fast forward to 2018, and *NXT TakeOver* is one of the hottest tickets in town. In a weekend known for over-the-top spectacle, NXT is all about the wrestling, and it's the show hardcore fans have been salivating to see. Headlined by the very personal rivalry (and unsanctioned match) between Johnny Gargano and Tommaso Ciampa; a Six-Man Ladder Match to determine the first-ever NXT North American Championship; the finals of the Dusty Rhodes Classic; and championship matches between Aleister Black and Andrade "Cien" Almas, and Shanya Baszler and Ember Moon, the capacity crowd of 13,955 inside the Smoothie King Center witnessed what many feel was the best pure wrestling show during *WrestleMania* weekend. Every match on the card lived up to the hype, with Black defeating Almas to capture the NXT Championship, former MMA fighter Baszler locking in a rear naked choke to defeat Moon to win the NXT Women's Championship, and Roderick Strong joining The Undisputed ERA to help the heel group take home the Dusty Rhodes Classic trophy. At the end of the night, though, it was the spectacular (and personal) 37-minute unsanctioned match between Gargano and Ciampa and the Six-Man Ladder Match that received the most buzz, leaving a lot to live up to for those in the matches on the main roster of *WrestleMania*.

"Triple H loves when NXT steals the weekend," laughs Ricochet, a recently signed highflyer who competed in the breathtaking and bruise-making Ladder Match. Working through the particulars of the match at the Performance Center, Ricochet said that the coaching staff on hand, including Shawn Michaels (who helped introduce the WWE Universe to Ladder Matches in *WrestleMania X*) and head coach Matt Bloom (formerly known as Lord Tensai and Prince Albert), had big things in mind for the introduction of the North American Championship. "Shawn and Coach Bloom really want to be hands-on," he explains. "They keep saying that they want this to be the best match of the weekend. Whether it's *TakeOver* or *Mania*, they want this to be the best match, so they're fully invested in this. Just that alone is so cool."

Match participants included Ricochet, EC3, Killian Dain, Lars Sullivan, Velveteen Dream, and the eventual winner, Adam Cole (bay-bay!), and the show opener proved to be a show stealer with a combination of gravity-defying and ladder-smashing moments that left the crowd breathless as they chanted "This is awesome!" while watching Ricochet's dangerous acrobatics, including him hitting a moonsault off a falling ladder. "If we just did a six-man match, that would be cool too, but the ladders add an element of surprise, an element of suspense, and an extra element of danger," says Ricochet. "The WWE Universe loves the image of us throwing ladders in the ring and climbing the ladders and flying off of them." Ricochet, who has been known for flying off the top rope since he started wrestling back in high school in 2003, says he is living his dream through NXT, as it was his goal since day one to reach WWE. "I started wrestling when I was fifteen," he

says. "I would do it on the weekends for fun. I got to hang out with some cool people and it was awesome. When I graduated from high school, I started working in a factory with my mom. It was a fiber glass factory, and it was hot and sticky and itchy . . . just horrible. I hated it. We worked ten-hour days, Monday through Thursday, but we had the three-day weekends off, so I could wrestle Saturday and Sunday, get back Monday morning, and go straight to work. In 2010, I got offered to go to Japan. So I put in my two weeks' notice at work, and they told me they would always take me back. I thought it was perfect, thinking I'd eventually go back to work, but I went to Japan and I guess they really liked me — I haven't had another job since. It was pretty rough for a while, money-wise, but it was a cool experience and I wouldn't change it for the world. Luckily, once I started making a name for myself, I got an agent who helped me out with bookings. He would take care of everything: the booking, the lodging, the travel, and he really helped me out a lot."

In 2013, Ricochet received his first tryout with WWE, but he didn't get signed. "Looking back, I'm kind of glad they didn't sign me because I was inexperienced," he admits. "I don't think I was ready, and I think they could sense that. After I didn't get signed, that's when I really found myself and became who I am today."

Ricochet headed to Japan, performed in independent shows, donned a mask, and went by the name Prince Puma in Lucha Underground, before eventually reaching out to William Regal of NXT to see if he could get another shot at that elusive WWE contract. Says Ricochet, "I felt like it was just time. If I didn't go now, it would be a wasted opportunity. It's been a dream since I was a kid to be here, so when I was free of all of my other contracts, it just felt right. NXT is at the forefront of sports-entertainment. Just look at the roster. The whole roster of NXT is awesome, and that's another reason why I thought right now was the perfect time to go."

On January 16, 2018, WWE made the official announcement that Ricochet had signed and would be joining the NXT roster. A few weeks later, he was shown in the crowd during *NXT TakeOver: Philadelphia*, and the Universe went absolutely nuts. "I was out in the crowd watching Johnny and Andrade's match, and you could feel the electricity pulsating out of people," he says. "One thing about the NXT crowd, they know how to get loud in a hurry."

After joining the NXT roster, Ricochet reported to the Performance Center to train with the various coaches before making his on-screen debut. "Oh man, the place is so cool," Ricochet says with a laugh. "I've been there for three months now, and even today, I walked in and I was in awe — the place is just so cool. It doesn't get old walking in there and seeing all of the rings and seeing all of the people . . . it has such a good energy and such a good vibe. We have everything at our disposal. We have the coolest training room, we have seven wrestling rings to do our thing in, and everything else we could ever want or need at our fingertips.

"When I got first got there, I started in Robbie Brookside's class. I can't say enough nice things about Brookside. He's so cool. He's so patient with everyone. After about a month or two, I moved up to Scotty 2 Hotty's class, and that was really cool for me. He really helped me out with a lot of small things that I never really thought about. About a month after that, I got moved up to Shawn Michael's class. So now, I'm sitting there with Michaels and we're watching old tapes and watching old *Raw* matches, and there's so much knowledge and wisdom in what he has to say about every match, every move. He has different people in his class, and he understands everyone's style, he understands everyone's character, and he's not afraid to work with us. If we have questions, or if we want to stay after, he'll stay after."

And Michaels's ability to teach to different styles has Ricochet really excited, especially since the man formerly known as King Ricochet possesses a style all his own. "You're watching something that you've never seen before," he says, when asked to describe his style to the WWE Universe. "I feel like I'm the perfect hybrid of many styles. I do a lot of things people think isn't even possible. I feel like I'm watching something you've never seen before, but you're seeing it happen right before your eyes."

One thing the WWE Universe shouldn't expect to see, however, is his popular Prince Puma mask making an appearance. "When I did Lucha Underground, that was all their character," he says. "I had no control over that character. Prince Puma was their idea, their design, their mask. They came at me for a good couple of months, but I kept saying no. Finally, they offered me a pretty good deal, so I thought I'm still pretty young, I can try this for a couple of years, so I took the chance. When I was on the indies, I had people come up to me, who knew me only as Prince Puma, so I thought it was cool that the promotion brought some new eyes on me. But I don't plan on bringing the mask back to NXT. How could I cover up this beautiful face?"

CHAPTER 34
205 Live

The *WrestleMania* pre-show included the surprising return of Bray Wyatt helping Woken Matt Hardy win the fifth annual Andre the Giant Memorial Battle Royal, as well as Bayley taking out Sasha Banks before being eliminated by Naomi to win the first-ever Women's *WrestleMania* Battle Royal. But it was Cedric Alexander versus Mustafa Ali for the Cruiserweight Championship who had the most to prove, not only for themselves but for the *205 Live* brand.

205 Live was rocked with uncertainty earlier in the year when then Cruiserweight champ Enzo Amore was released. The brand hit reset, not only on-screen with new General Manager Drake Maverick, but behind the scenes, as Triple H took a more active role in running the show. "Honestly, Triple H's help has really given us the edge we needed," says Alexander. "I always felt like we were just missing a key component to help set us apart from *Raw* and *SmackDown*. By making us more in-ring focused, more like NXT, we've taken that step forward. To me, I felt like the in-ring style has always been top-notch, and now that the emphasis for *205 Live* is that in-ring action, it has helped set us apart as our own brand, instead of just being a smaller version of *Raw*. *205 Live* has grown by leaps and bounds — we went from being the new kids on the block and a brand that people didn't want to invest in to one of the hottest brands in the company."

While Amore was champion, his reign caused friction backstage, but the other *205 Live* talent tried to make the best of the situation. "Enzo wasn't necessarily a mat tactician like most of us are," says Alexander. "We are all independent wrestling guys who love wrestling and that was our niche, whether we were highflyers or ground-based guys or hard hitters and kickers like Hideo Itami. Enzo didn't really fit any of those molds. He was more of a character-based guy. He stuck out, some positive ways, some negative ways, but everyone came at it like, 'We got what we got, now it's time to make it work.'"

After Amore was fired, the brand went back to what the WWE Universe wanted from the cruiserweights: fast-paced, high-flying action. To crown a new champ, WWE announced a championship tournament, with the finals playing out at *WrestleMania*. "For months, people had been talking behind the scenes, like, 'Wouldn't it be great if they did another Cruiserweight Classic,'" says Alexander. "We were hoping they'd make it an annual tournament. So when they announced this tournament, we were like, 'Okay, this is a chance to give it a Cruiserweight Classic feel,' especially in this rebranding phase where we're trying to reshape the division. This was a perfect way to crown a new champ, but going back to the same way we started. We started as a classic wrestling tournament and that's what our fans want to see. They don't want to see a bunch of character-driven skits. The *205 Live* audience wants to see straight wrestling, and the tournament delivered."

Wrestling in front of over 75,000 fans, Alexander and Ali hit the pre-show in full stride, delivering an exciting final that saw Alexander crowned as the new champ. "Me and Mustafa are two sides of the same coin," says Alexander. "No matter how small our moment, it doesn't matter, we don't care what spot we have on the card, our intent is to steal the show. We want to make such an impression that when the night is over, fans are still talking about our match. And there's no better time than *WrestleMania* for us to turn it up to eleven and make sure the WWE Universe walks away with something to remember. Last year, I missed *WrestleMania*, and it was something that really weighed heavy on me. I was happy to be a part of the company, I was happy to be a part of *WrestleMania* in general, but knowing that I could've been in the ring that night . . . I was sidelined because of my knee injury, it really tore me up. It gave me more motivation to be on the *WrestleMania 34* card, and now here I am."

It shows just how far Alexander has come, as he walked into the Cruiserweight Classic back in 2016 as an unsigned talent just hoping to make a name for himself. Alexander did just that, putting on a classic match against Kota Ibushi that led to one of the biggest, most genuinely heartfelt crowd reactions WWE has seen in years, with fans in attendance showering Alexander (and the powers that be backstage) with chants of "Please sign Cedric!"

"That was a huge surprise to me," says Alexander. "I did not see that coming. Going into the tournament, I was kind of a known name on the indies, and I thought maybe I'd be a name some people might recognize, but I don't think anybody expected, in 2016, for me and Kota Ibushi to have one of the top five matches of that year. It blew my mind. I didn't expect to get the reaction that I did. I went in with the mindset I always have, and that's to make sure I make an impression. Win, lose, or draw, I felt in my heart that I was going to walk out with something. To get the ovation that I did, I felt like I was solidifying my name as one of the top professionals in the world. To this day, I still can't believe I got that type of reaction on my second WWE match."

After the match, Triple H added to the hype, as he put his arm around the young cruiserweight and let him know that he had indeed made it to the big time. "It was like you just got the game-winning touchdown and your dad is so proud of you . . . it was that type of feeling," laughs Alexander. "I remember after the match was over, I was a

big ball of emotions. As I was leaving the ring and headed backstage, I heard the WWE Universe lose their minds over this match. It was crazy. Then as I got to the back, the guys who were going on after me — Akira Tozawa, Jack Gallagher, and Tommaso Ciampa — were like, 'That's exactly what you needed. It was flawless!' And as I was sitting there losing my mind in emotions and tears, Triple H walked up to me, put his arm around my head, and told me, 'That was great, that was beautiful. Go back out for a curtain call.'

"In my head, I was like, 'Only top guys get curtain calls. Why would I get a curtain call?' But when I went out there, it was like three or four minutes of people chanting 'Please sign Cedric!' It was the loudest reaction I ever heard. It still gives me chills thinking about it. Once Triple H came back, he pretty much solidified my signing and he shook my hand and told me how great it was. Then, right before he walked back to the production area, he stopped, looked in my eyes, and said, 'Welcome to the family.' My heart dropped. I just got the sign-off by the man himself. I was part of the family now. It's something I'll never forget."

CHAPTER 35
Eat, Sleep, *WrestleMania*, Repeat

APRIL 8, 2018: *WRESTLEMANIA 34*

Blood. Betrayal. Beat downs. *WrestleMania 34* featured a little bit of everything, from Finn Bálor's entrance alongside members of the New Orleans LGBTQ community to The Queen's reign over The Empress in what is arguably the best Women's Championship Match in *WrestleMania* history. Braun Strowman pulled a ten-year-old kid named Nicholas (the son of a WWE official) from the crowd to be his tag team partner, then proceeded to upset The Bar and snatch their gold. Daniel Bryan returned to the thunderous chants of "Yes! Yes! Yes!" And Seth Rollins won the Intercontinental Championship in a Triple Threat for the ages. Nia Jax took down her bully, The Bludgeon Brothers lived up to their name, Jinder Mahal proved that he wasn't through winning titles, and AJ Styles defeated The King of Strong Style only to be hit with a low blow and a congratulatory Nakamura heel turn. Undertaker even decided to cut his retirement short, squashing John Cena in under three minutes before raising a fist to the appreciative crowd of 78,133. The biggest surprise of the night, however, was the eye-popping performance of Ronda Rousey in what was universally heralded as the match of the night. Rousey eclipsed all expectations, stealing the show while cementing her spot among the must-see acts in WWE.

"After my wedding day, this is my favorite day of my life," a tearful Rousey told WWE.com cameras moments after her match. "This is what she was meant to do," added her *WrestleMania* tag team partner, Kurt Angle. "You saw it out there, that's her first match. Look how she blew the roof off that joint."

But as loud as the crowd was in cheering Rousey, they expressed their feelings about the Reigns and Lesnar main event even more vocally. After a year of building Reigns up for his crowning achievement and championship moment, the crowd revolted. And no matter how many F5s and German suplexes Reigns kicked out of, he was booed, until finally Lesnar busted the Big Dog open with a shocking series of ground-and-pound elbow strikes before delivering a devastating sixth F5 to finally finish off the crimson masked Superstar. Paul Heyman was right (again!) with his "that's not a prediction, it's a spoiler" statement. And just like when Lesnar upset Undertaker to become the one in 21–1, the crowd walked out of the Superdome stunned and in total disbelief over what they just witnessed. With Lesnar's contract expiring, just about everyone in the building went into the match believing Reigns would walk out of New Orleans as the champ. But Vince McMahon had other things in mind. It was a secret so big, only a few insiders knew the outcome before the pin. Not even the creative team knew Lesnar was keeping the title. The next day brought an even bigger surprise: Lesnar had not only re-signed with WWE, but he'd be defending his Universal Championship against Reigns in a rematch at the *Greatest Royal Rumble* event in Saudi Arabia on a stacked card that also featured a 50-man Royal Rumble, Triple H versus John Cena, and Undertaker taking on Rusev in a Casket Match. Less than 24 hours after *WrestleMania 34*, and the storytelling machine that is Vince McMahon and WWE had already turned the page to the next chapter in their never-ending, between-the-ropes adventure.

"There's no off-season for the talent or for the creative team," says Brian James. "*WrestleMania* is just so special for everyone involved, and you try to put together the best show possible, but then everyone heads to the after party, and within hours, you're already thinking about the *Raw* and *SmackDown* after *Mania*. What surprises can we bring to those shows? What stories are we carrying over from *Mania*? Where do we go from here? You're so proud of your work as you watch it play out, but at the same time, in the back of your mind, you're already coming up with ideas on how to make it even bigger and better."

So what exactly would a "bigger and better" *WrestleMania 35* look like? Seth Rollins is hoping for a shot at the Universal Championship in a Triple Threat featuring all three members of The Shield. The Miz is looking forward to the showdown brewing between himself and Daniel Bryan. But those aren't the only possibilities being talked about. Will we see the first-ever women's main event featuring Ronda Rousey taking on Charlotte Flair? Maybe a return to another classic from outside of WWE, with AJ Styles versus Samoa Joe? Or could the main

event feature a true David versus Goliath battle between Daniel Bryan and either Brock Lesnar or Braun Strowman? Or maybe, just maybe, Roman Reigns will finally embrace the boos and return the hate, calling out his cousin Dwayne "The Rock" Johnson for an epic clash . . .

"I think he'd be down for it," says Reigns. "I know family is just so important to him, and that brotherhood and that camaraderie is an integral part of who we are, even within your bloodline. I look at my cousins, The Usos, and I don't look at them as my cousins, I look at them as if they are my blood brothers. It would obviously be a good draw, it would make money, and there's no doubt it would sell tickets. It just depends on what type of story we would tell, what kind of rivalry we want, and the reason we'd be fighting. There are a lot of details and a lot of ground we'd need to lay down before we could really get there, but if it's good for the business, if it's good for my career, I don't see why not. If it's all positive and he's with it, I'll take a slap punch. Rock Bottom me, baby . . . just let me kick out at two."

SPECIAL THANKS

To me, *WrestleMania 2* was a show of firsts. It was the first pay-per-view I ever ordered. First time I ever saw a Steel Cage Match. First time seeing The British Bulldogs. I was hooked. Never would I have guessed that 32 years later, my love of wrestling would lead me to writing a book on *WrestleMania 34*, watching alongside my daughter, her eyes as wide as mine were back in the day when Hulk Hogan dropped the leg on King Kong Bundy for the epic win. Thanks to Caroline for being by my side during every pay-per-view. Thanks to Brenden for his reactions during every kendo stick swing on Xavier Woods. And thanks to Nicole, the Vince McMahon of our house, who always knows what's best for business. Special thanks, as always, to the men and women of WWE who continue to travel over 200 days a year to entertain millions around the globe, while, at the same time, taking time out from their car, their home, or while eating backstage to talk to me for this book. Last but not least, this book could not have been written without the help of Steve Pantaleo, who never guessed when he assigned me the book that I was going to ask to interview just about everybody on the roster, and it was up to him to make it happen. Talk about work rate. He is five star all the way.

—JON ROBINSON